PLAYING
GOD
IN CHAIR
TWELVE

To my beloved ♡ B

PLAYING
GOD
IN CHAIR
TWELVE

A JUROR'S

FAITH-CHANGING

JOURNEY

CARL DUBLER

Playing God in Chair Twelve: A Juror's Faith-Changing Journey
Published by Golden Elm Press
Boulder, CO

Although the author and publisher have made every effort to ensure that the information in this book was correct at press time, the author and publisher do not assume and hereby disclaim any liability to any party for any loss, damage, or disruption caused by errors or omissions, whether such errors or omissions result from negligence, accident, or any other cause.

Publisher's Cataloging-in-Publication data

Names: Dubler, Carl, author.
Title: Playing God in chair twelve : a juror's faith-changing journey / by Carl Dubler.
Description: First trade paperback original edition. | Boulder [Colorado] : Golden Elm Press, 2019. Also published as an ebook.
Identifiers: ISBN 978-1-7325292-0-5
Subjects: LCSH: Jury—Religious aspects—Christianity. | Jury—United States—Decision making. | Trials (Murder)—Colorado.
BISAC: BIOGRAPHY & AUTOBIOGRAPHY / Personal Memoirs.
Classification: LCC KF221.M8 | DDC 345–dc22

Cover by Victoria Wolf
Interior design by Andrea Costantine

QUANTITY PURCHASES: Schools, companies, professional groups, clubs, churches and other organizations may qualify for special terms when ordering quantities of this title. For information, email info@goldenelmpress.com.

Scripture quotations taken from the New American Standard Bible® (NASB), Copyright © 1960, 1962, 1963, 1968, 1971, 1972, 1973, 1975, 1977, 1995 by The Lockman Foundation. Used by permission. www.Lockman.org

To people of courage, especially my wife.

PROLOGUE

You are reading this book because of a court order. In 2018, the five-lawyer appeals team for a convicted double-murderer discovered, by accident, that I had written this book after serving on the jury that convicted their client.

At that time, the book had yet to be published, so they had no idea what was in it. Naturally, they wanted to see if anything in the book might help their appeal. Amazingly, the appellate court agreed they should see it, and I was forced to hand it over and spend a day answering questions in court. This was as stressful as it was rare. I'm not sure anything like this had ever happened before—calling a juror nearly a decade after trial to testify, based on his unpublished book, in the appeals case of the man he voted to convict.

I wrote the book as a way of processing the ten-week trial, the subsequent verdicts, and how it all changed my life. I was trying to redeem the experience and make something good of it. Over the years, what started as a messy draft of recollections took shape into a book. Sometimes I would write feverishly for several days. A year could go by too when I wouldn't even touch it. At times I loved what I wrote, but I often hated confronting the feelings it raised in me. Sometimes I truly believed the world should hear my story, and other times I wanted to throw the whole thing away and forget any of it ever happened.

Nine years later, my manuscript remained unpublished. As I sat on the witness stand answering questions in front of the man I had judged, I had a clarifying moment: if bits and pieces of my story—the parts the appeals team deemed beneficial—was going to be forced into the open anyway, I might as well publish it. All of it.

This book depicts actual events as truthfully as I can recall or verify by research. Occasionally, I've supplemented dialogue for clarity or to help explain a scene but kept it consistent with the character or nature of the person speaking. Everyone in my story is an actual person; there are no composite characters. I've changed the name of some individuals to respect their privacy. It is also important to remember that I am writing about my experience looking back after many years and often summarize events to simplify confusing timelines.

Until I faced the reality of murder head-on as a juror, I didn't understand how deeply a single murder, not to mention multiple murders, affected the lives of hundreds of people. As a juror and now witness, I have been called a racist and a religious bigot by those who disagreed with my decisions. Others have called me courageous, engaging, and inspirational. Some have said that I reflect an ugly ignorance. Yet at the same time, others have lauded me for bettering humanity.

I'll leave it to you to decide which of these things is true, if any at all. What I know for sure is this: I'm not the same man I was before.

one

THE JUDGMENT SEAT

For the first time, I allowed myself a good, long look at the man I was to judge. Most people called him *the defendant.* His trial had entered its tenth week. The action in the courtroom that day was beset with delays, with the lawyers constantly stopping to argue procedural issues with the judge. They huddled tip-toe at the judge's bench, whispering their arguments, the judge covering the microphone with his hand because the jurors weren't supposed to hear them. Over the past two months, I'd learned the more the lawyers strained to stay in a whisper during those bench conferences, the more likely we'd be escorted out, so the lawyers could properly yell at each other before the judge. During this particular delay, the whispering reached about thirty percent of maximum—hardly notable. I watched the defendant instead.

I was sitting in what we jurors called the courtside seats. The jury box in courtroom 201 in the Arapahoe County Justice Center in Colorado was not big enough for a jury of twenty (there were eight alternates), so we took turns sitting in black leather chairs set outside the jury box on the main floor of the courtroom. They were more comfortable than the worn, blue fabric chairs inside the box, but nobody liked those courtside seats where we sat exposed without a bannister, railing, or anything to hide behind. Outside the protection of the jury box, I sat directly at eye-level with the defendant, close enough to see he was drawing on scrap paper.

It looked like he was drawing a series of shapes: rectangles, triangles, and circles. He bit his lower lip in concentration as he drew. Did he care that I would soon decide his fate? Did he realize I was watching him? The defendant didn't seem particularly interested in me, despite the power I had over him. The few fleeting times we made eye contact, we both looked away, like two reluctant acquaintances pretending not to notice each other at a party. I sat in the middle of a crowded, windowless courtroom bathed in fluorescent light and pondered condemning him to death. He sat before me scribbling on paper.

I glanced down at my official juror notebook. I, too, scribbled during the frequent delays in the trial. There in the margins I drew a series of three-dimensional shapes—cubes, pyramids, cylinders—trying to occupy my mind during breaks in the action.

A question began to nag me: is it possible that my mind worked the same way as the defendant's? I didn't want this to be true. The defendant was a drug dealer who had been sentenced to over eighty years of prison time for other crimes and now sat before me as a convicted murderer. He used his considerable intellect for criminal enterprise, while I used mine to build a successful career in computer software. He grew up in the urban jungle of Chicago's South Side, learning from his older brothers how to cut and bundle marijuana for sale. I came from a small town at the foot of Colorado's Rocky Mountains, singing in the church choir and getting straight-As.

We were not at all alike—except that we both scribbled to give shape to our wandering thoughts. We both liked to keep things clean and organized on our desks (he would frequently line up pens and pencils neatly in front of him). We also both had a cool and dispassionate demeanor. I never once saw him react emotionally to anything, even in the face of damning testimony from his former friends. He never flinched even when autopsy photos of the dead were shown, their naked bodies cold and stiff on a stainless-steel table. If our minds did operate in the same way, what then was the real difference between us? If I had been raised in his circumstances and he in mine, would we be in different seats in this courtroom?

This is exactly how the defense attorneys wanted me to think. That were it not for the random circumstances of birth, any of us could become a criminal. They said I should choose mercy because of this. Then I looked at the other side of the courtroom, to the prosecutors and the families of the victims. These people suffered more than the loss of a child, sibling, or friend. They had waited more than four years for justice and wanted me to uphold the standards of the community. The defendant was a murderer, and—they emphasized—not everyone who grows up in a bad neighborhood ends up with that title. My mind wavered between the hopelessly conflicted ideals of justice and mercy. Maybe I was not prepared to handle the task of being an actual judge, even with my years of preparation in the evangelical church.

◆　◆　◆

I didn't intend to become the type of Christian many people complain about—arrogant, self-righteous, judgmental. It happened gradually over many years, building on layer after layer of sermons on sin. I dutifully protected myself against sin, wearing a bulky suit of spiritual armor to keep the arrows of temptation from piercing me. As I grew to adulthood, I became proud of how tough my armor was. I had the strength to avoid the snares of the devil, whether it be drinking, premarital sex, or any other earthly delights. When others struggled with the consequences of sin, my automatic, subconscious reaction was not to help or sympathize. I did not respond with an act of grace. Instead, I wondered aloud why they hadn't the good sense to armor themselves in the first place, steeling themselves against sin. Like I did. Then, shortly after my thirty-eighth birthday, I was thrust into the ordeal of jury service that suddenly revealed to me the type of Christian I had become.

The case before me was a notorious double murder that badly shook the community. The trial had two parts. First, the guilt phase, where those of us on the jury needed to determine if the defendant was guilty of the murders. If guilty, the sentencing phase came next to determine his punishment. The entire process took ten weeks of my life in 2009.

The district attorney was seeking the death penalty. Under Colorado law, death can only be imposed by the same jury that found the defendant guilty of the murder. The law places this life-or-death decision in the hands of criminal justice amateurs.

Initially, I thought that I would be very anxious to get this ordeal over and done. But as the weeks wore on, I actually came to dread the end of the trial and facing the ultimate decision, whether to sentence the defendant to life in prison or death row. How could I ever be ready to make such a choice?

The courtroom, though, was packed with people waiting for my decision and directly affected by it. There were the family members of the murder victims. They sat in the front row of the courtroom every day, turning their pained faces away when detectives showed pictures of the bloody crime scene, or when attorneys held up sealed plastic evidence bags with items taken off the bodies of their loved ones—a torn and blood-stained shirt, a wallet, eyeglasses. There was an endless parade of police officers and detectives who invested their careers in the case. They testified wearily, sighing, explaining yet again some tiny detail they pored over many times before. There were the attorneys, who wheeled-in luggage carts stacked with three-ring binders containing thousands of pages of case notes. There was a phalanx of reporters anxious for anything newsworthy to report, especially a verdict. They came to the courtroom each day unsure of whether to sit on the defendant's or prosecution's side of the room. And, of course, there was the defendant himself, whose life depended upon what I decided. All these people looked at me expectantly every time I arrived in the courtroom and stood whenever I entered or exited.

I was new to this experience. The pressure of a life-altering decision. The responsibility of seeing that justice was done. People standing whenever I entered or exited a room. The judge said that they stood as a sign of respect for the authority that we citizen-jurors were granted. I didn't think of it that way. When everyone in the courtroom stood, I saw it as a signal they weren't going to sit around forever. They wanted something—a decision from me in their favor. And they were tired of waiting for it. I wondered if they stood in anticipation, not respect.

I reacted to all that pressure and authority in unusual ways. After one particularly troubling day, I hurried to my car as quickly as I could and drove away with a twitchy foot on the gas pedal and a ball of tension rising from my gut. I am normally a quiet and reserved person, not prone to emotional outbursts of any kind. My friends and family, even my own wife, need to ask me if I am feeling excited, worried, or sad about something because they cannot tell simply by looking at me. I would make a great poker player if it weren't such a sin to gamble.

It startled me as the tension squeezed up into my throat and burst out into a half yell, half scream. I braced my arms against the steering wheel as I took in a quick breath and the sound came out again. No words, just a loud, primal yell as though I were about to charge down a hill and into battle. This happened again on a few other days as I drove home. I wanted to yell. I needed to yell. But first, a quick look around to see if any other drivers would see or even hear me yelling. It might make me feel better for a few minutes, but this new and bizarre behavior scared me.

I dealt with stressful situations before with incredible calm, a trait that earned me the nickname "Iceman" from some of my college friends. I remember being a student pilot at age nineteen, flying a small airplane solo for the first time and looking down a thousand feet at the runway. I felt a twinge of alarm when the reality set in that I was the only person who could land the plane. Then I simply reassured myself that I knew what I was doing and landed the plane. In high school and college, I competed in public speaking and debate contests, something that terrifies most people. I won a collegiate regional championship in a style of debate where the topic, and what side I was to argue, were announced only five minutes beforehand. I even once stared down a snarling Rottweiler dog that charged at me, my wife, and baby daughter as we were out for a walk. I distracted the dog away from my little family while I looked for a rock or anything to use as a weapon. In those five or ten seconds as the dog approached, spittle flying from its jaws, I was calm enough to determine that I should sacrifice my feet before my hands, since I needed my hands more for work. Fortunately, at that moment, a car drove by slowly and the dog lunged at the driver's open window, biting the rear-view mirror on the door before running off.

Never in my life had I shown nerves, much less yelled. I didn't panic in the airplane or at the podium. I didn't even yell at the Rottweiler. But now, what was I becoming? Why was this trial so difficult? For my entire life, I'd been so certain of everything. This explained my calmness. It was easy to be calm when I knew the right answer to anything.

Right and wrong behavior? Got it.

Good versus evil? No problem.

The will of God? I could tell you what it is.

That day, my new reaction to the stress of the trial made me wonder if I really did have any answers.

◆ ◆ ◆

We were nearing the end of the trial on the day when I watched the defendant drawing at his desk. I lowered my tall frame into the car with a heaviness that made my knees creak and just sat in quiet for a minute. What did it matter what I chose to do? I could choose mercy and offend everyone who clamored for the full extent of justice. Or I could choose the death penalty and offend everyone who said that there had already been enough tears, suffering, and death. Either way, I was going to anger a large group of people and bring even more grief and misery into their lives. Justice. Mercy. Kill him. Spare him.

I let out a long breath and started my car. As I drove home, the people in my suburban world around me attended to the mundane details of life—preparing a family meal, helping children with schoolwork, watching television. I imagined there were many dinnertime conversations starting with, "How was your day?" I, however, could tell no one my thoughts, prohibited by the judge from discussing any aspect of the trial with anyone—even my wife. The world around me continued with its busywork, oblivious to my life-or-death decision.

The uncharacteristic yelling I had experienced gave way to a quiet loneliness, the outbursts of stress yielding to a depressed resignation. The time for final judgment had come. It had been ten weeks since the trial began, four years since the defendant was arrested, and five years since the tragedy that would eventually bring us all together ripped apart the tranquility of a mild summer evening.

two
The Ghost of Gregory Vann

I got my first glimpse of this case, which would become my new job of judgment, from the news on July 5, 2004. The previous day, my family and I attended an Independence Day celebration at a city park, complete with patriotic music playing from a bandstand. Hundreds of people sat on lawn chairs and blankets as we waited for the fireworks, the sky turning from blue to orange to black behind the tall mountain peaks just west of Denver. While we watched the fireworks, my toddler-age son hid under a blanket to escape the noise, and a young man named Gregory Vann was shot and killed at another park ten miles away. Two other young men, Javad Fields and Elvin Bell, survived their gunshot wounds. According to the newscast, police were still searching for two suspects.

I never encountered crime like this in my part of town. My young family lived in the suburbs of Denver. I was certainly the typical suburbanite, with very few real troubles, far away from the trials and tribulations that

I imagined characterized some urban areas. My worst offense had been a traffic ticket, I'd never been caught trespassing, had no tattoos, and couldn't identify the smell of marijuana. What passed as major controversy in my software business was requiring people to have passwords of eight characters instead of merely six. Adventures at home might include the volcano science project for my daughter's third-grade class or fixing the broken sprinkler head in the lawn.

I would have felt out of place among the dozens of black teenagers at Lowry Park on that balmy July Fourth evening. The teens were gathered for a rap contest and barbeque. Although I was in my late thirties by the time the trial began, African-Americans were almost completely unknown to me. I grew up in and around Fort Collins, a quiet town known as the "Choice City of Colorado" for its mild climate and beautiful scenery at the base of the Rocky Mountains. The orderly, well-planned town had been settled by hard-working German immigrants and had wide, tree-lined streets. The relentlessly conservative politics of the area led some to joke that Fort Collins was "the city of wide streets and narrow minds." Almost everyone who lived there was white.

Even still, my life was not completely devoid of diversity. When I was fourteen, I lived for a summer in a poor neighborhood in Guadalajara, Mexico where there were no other Americans or English speakers. In college, I played on a soccer team composed of Muslims from Southwest Asia and North Africa. I was the only white person and Christian on the team. But I don't remember meeting a black person until I was a student at Colorado State University. In addition, I knew only one as a coworker in the first part of my career in the computer software business. Simply put, there were more African-Americans at Lowry Park that fateful evening than I had met in my entire life.

Calling Lowry Park in Aurora, Colorado, a "park" was a bit of an overstatement. Perched on the edge of an abandoned Air Force base, it consisted of a parking lot, picnic pavilion, a patch of grass, some pine trees, and a portable restroom in the middle of a parched field. The grass there was green, as long as it grew in the area where the sprinklers reached. The young people had met at the pavilion that July Fourth evening. They were loud and raucous and enjoying themselves. Each young man there dressed in enough fabric to make two outfits. They wore pants a couple sizes too large and cinched well below the waist. Jerseys representing their favorite teams or players hung past the waist to mid-thigh, making up for any gap in coverage. A logoed baseball cap was on every head, usually twisted sideways or backwards.

If what the boys wore could be described as oversized, quite the opposite could be said for the young ladies of the group. They made up for the excessive use of clothing on the guys by wearing as little of it as possible themselves. Their wardrobe was a study of impossibilities. Impossibly short shorts. Impossibly deep necklines. Impossibly high heels. Impossibly large earrings. The girls arrived at the event teetering on their heels and shimmering in gold fabrics. This wasn't a group for the shy. Loud and bold was the way to go, and your talk and your walk had to be full of youthful swagger.

I would see all this on videos captured by those who were there and entered as evidence in the trial. If I had been there, I can only imagine how awkward I would have felt, especially because the highlight of the evening was a rap contest. To succeed at freestyle rap, you need a natural sense of rhythm, the creativity to rhyme on-the-fly, and the confidence to grab the microphone and take charge, even if you didn't exactly know what you were going to say. These aren't the skill sets of my polo shirt and khaki pants world of software engineering.

Three young men ran the show that evening: Gregory (Greg) Vann, his brother Elvin Bell, and their friend Javad Marshall Fields. Greg and Javad had just finished their junior year of college, and they filled their summers with various business activities to earn money for school. For two prior Independence Days, they ran the All-City Barbeque and Rap Contest at Lowry Park as partners in a small business they called We Are Real Entertainment.

Javad strode among the crowd, part referee and part cheerleader for the various rap contestants who strutted to the microphone. Each rap followed a template of sorts: brag about your own amazing exploits and then take a swipe at your rivals, especially those who were at the microphone just before you. The typical menu of exploits to brag about included all the money you've spent, cars you've owned, your "crib" (I've since learned that this is one's house), the girls you've been with, the fights you've won, the turf you control, and your general awesomeness. You had to do it all in rhyme and while staying on rhythm. If you ran short on words, especially adjectives, there was a handy all-purpose alternative: *motherfuckin'*. If you didn't know quite what to call something, you could call it *shit*. So, to express amazement at something that was just beyond the reach of your daily lexicon, you could simply say, *Man, that motherfuckin' shit is fucked up!*

During each rap, the crowd would hoot and holler, and good riffs got big yells and laughs as they tossed their heads back and stomped on the ground. Javad could barely be heard even with a microphone as he attempted to take votes on who had the best rap. I saw energy under that pavilion, and a spark that made even an unattractive place like Lowry Park come alive. More than race or socioeconomic background, this would have made me feel the most out of place. These kids were having fun, and fun was something I didn't know how to do.

Growing up as an evangelical Christian, I learned early on that what the rest of the world calls "fun" is actually "sin." Not all Christians are like this, but my church was one of the more conservative, fundamentalist types. Growing up, I learned that there was a definite right and wrong answer to everything.

Creationism is right, evolution is wrong.

Long hair or pierced ears don't belong on men.

Christians shouldn't watch R-rated movies.

Christians shouldn't listen to "worldly" music like pop or rock-and-roll.

The more fun it seemed, the more dangerous it was: gambling, drinking, dancing, and sex. Especially sex. If there was an unforgivable sin, it was fornication—premarital sex.

To keep from falling into such temptations, I busied myself with righteous achievements. I was a top student in school and a good athlete. I became a computer wunderkind, beginning a career in the computer business at age sixteen and earning enough money to put myself through college. I started teaching computer classes at age seventeen for business people who paid to attend. Outside of the nascent computer industry, I loved conquering big challenges, like riding my bike over Fall River Pass (elevation just over twelve thousand feet), or running a half mile in less than two minutes, or obtaining my pilot's license when I was still a teenager.

If there had been rap contests when I was a teenager, there's no way I would have participated, even if I had the skills. To my results-oriented mind, it would have been an unprofitable waste of time. Plus, there was simply too much swearing.

◆ ◆ ◆

The pavilion at Lowry Park was connected to the parking lot by a section of sidewalk about seventy-five feet long. At the point where the sidewalk meets the parking lot was a patch of grass and a small tree. This is where Greg Vann fell.

By all accounts, Greg was a friendly young man. At only five-feet, two-inches tall and barely one hundred thirty pounds, he was small for his twenty years, but that didn't dampen his enthusiasm. Pictures from earlier in the evening showed him striding across the parking lot, welcoming people to the show. He wore a big smile along with his oversized white pants, white tank top, and red plaid shirt, unbuttoned all the way down. His friend Javad worked in the spotlight, handling any job that required a microphone. Greg was a quieter person who didn't mind working behind-the-scenes logistics, like parking lot control.

That is why Greg got involved when, as the sun set below the purple mountain skyline, two young men came riding erratically across the dry grass in a gold Chevy Suburban, music blaring from the speakers. After swerving around the park and catching the attention of everyone, they stopped by the little tree next to the sidewalk, partially blocking the exit with their large vehicle. One of the two men had been at the party earlier in the day. He was a slender black man wearing a white jersey with the letters RWB on it, an acronym for *Are We Blazin'?*—slang for smoking marijuana.

On his first visit to the party, he had been drinking from a bottle of Courvoisier cognac. During the rap contest, he had yelled loudly, attracting dirty looks from the crowd. A woman with him had sheepishly told him to tone it down, and he left suddenly. Now, about an hour later, he was back, riding in a Suburban with a young black man with dreadlocks.

Greg approached the vehicle and asked that they move it out of the way of the exit. The request was not met with a friendly reply. The two men got out of the car and began yelling at Greg. Several of the other young men, including Javad and Elvin, left the pavilion and came running to investigate. A girl under the pavilion turned her video camera toward the emerging confrontation. Some people at the party began to leave, glancing over their shoulders as they walked briskly, fearing a fight was about to ensue. Words escalated into shouts and then into shoves. It was too late for a civil outcome now. The video showed the two young men from the Suburban lifting their shirts from the waist—a universal gang gesture to indicate they were armed. Sure enough, each had a semi-automatic pistol tucked in their waistbands.

These two men had already been carrying concealed weapons without permits. By lifting their shirts to show them off in a threatening manner, they now had committed the crime of menacing with a deadly weapon. Both actions were felonies in the State of Colorado.

Yet those two crimes were only a minor infraction not even worth prosecuting compared to the devastation that was about to ensue. As the two young men reached for their guns, nobody knew their actions were just the beginning of what would become a year of crime and terror. The killing that came next would only be a prelude.

At approximately 8:55 p.m., gunshots. Among screams of panic, the remaining crowd dispersed in all directions. Some ran into the dark, open field while others dove for cover behind parked cars. The two young men with guns jumped back into the gold Suburban and drove bouncing and scraping across the grass and into the night. Three young men laid on the ground, shot: Greg, Javad, and Elvin. Greg was not moving.

By the time Javad crawled over to him, Greg was probably dead. Javad tried CPR and continued with that effort until the police arrived a few minutes later. It was too late. Two .380 caliber gunshot wounds had pierced Greg near his shoulders, and the bullets traveled downward through his heart and lungs. It looked as if he had been shot from above, which wouldn't have been difficult given Greg's diminutive stature. Paramedics rushed Javad and Elvin to Denver Medical Center. Javad was shot in his left leg, just above the knee, and Elvin was shot in his right shoulder while another bullet grazed his throat, gouging out several layers of skin and leaving a bright red streak across the front of his neck. He was lucky to be alive.

The chaos eventually subsided, and yellow crime scene tape cordoned off the area. In the center of it all lay Greg Vann, flat on his back with his arms extended away from his body. His eyes, half shut, stared lifelessly up into the night sky. His mouth was open. It was not a bloody scene. His wounds were not even visible. His clothes were still on, except his baseball cap was laying on the grass near his head. His body would lay there until the morning while investigators took pictures and combed the area for evidence while the tree above him swayed softly in the breeze.

◆　◆　◆

While Greg lay dying, I was at the park on my side of town, ten miles away from Lowry Park. As Javad and Elvin were treated at the hospital, my wife and I walked home from our all-American celebration, our two young children in tow in a little red wagon. When I heard the news, I'm sure I didn't have much of a reaction. I likely paid little attention to the story. I heard something about Aurora and three people shot, one dead. I probably thought it sounded tragic and then quickly forgot about it the next day when a fresh batch of headline news arrived.

But for Javad Fields, who survived the shooting that night, the killing of his friend Gregory Vann soon set off a chain of events that would end his own life.

He would go to the police. He would identify one of the young men in that Chevy Suburban. He would agree to testify against that man. And when, after a year of bribery, intimidation, and threats, he refused to back away from testifying, the evening news reported more killing in Aurora. This time it was Javad Fields and his fiancé. Yet again, I saw headlines of young people dying in Aurora. But I didn't know that four years later, the entire saga would leave the realm of television news and become very real to me.

three
THE IDEAL CHRISTIAN BOY

Nothing about my childhood could have prepared me to deal head-on with murder. Where I grew up in Northern Colorado, crime was so rare, even a minor infraction would become a major cause for alarm. In 1981, when I was ten years old, a crime occurred that was nothing compared to murder, yet it would set the direction of my life for many years to come.

A teenage schoolmate named Gary was caught vandalizing cars at a dealership in town. Gary's father was on the board of elders at our church, like my own father. Somehow, Gary escaped any legal consequences for the damages he caused. But for a leader of a conservative, fundamentalist church like ours, an incident like this was much more serious than the mere legalities. The leaders of the evangelical church in that era had all come through the rebellious 1960s. The fundamentalism of the 1980s was a reaction to that. In our church, the Bible was the ultimate authority, with James Dobson of Focus on the Family and Bill Gothard, another famous authoritarian preacher of the era, coming in a close second. The Bible, in First Timothy chapter three, lists the qualifications for anyone who wants to be an elder in the church: "He must be one who manages his own household well, keeping his children under control with all dignity. If a man does not know how to manage his own household, how will he take care of the church of God?"

The elders reasoned that having a son who vandalizes cars is not keeping children under control with all dignity. They then judged that Gary's father was no longer qualified to be an elder, and he resigned.

Gary's father announced his resignation at a mid-week service, which we held on Thursday nights. Gary's father was a middle-aged man, with a slight frame and a bald head. He leaned on the side of the pulpit, a microphone in his right hand, his elbow tightly at his side. Standing on the stage a few steps above the congregation, he gazed up as though looking at something in the balcony.

"I am stepping down as an elder in the church," he began, tears forming. The congregation was quiet. I sat in a pew along the left edge of the sanctuary. I only glimpsed up at Gary's father once or twice. I leaned forward, my elbows on my knees, staring down at the floor in front of me. It was too painful and embarrassing to watch.

I'm sure that after the service there were plenty of assurances of prayers and support for Gary's father. That is how most Christians respond when faced with bad news. *I'll keep you in my prayers.* But for me, this became a vivid example of the pain an unruly son could bring to a father and an entire church.

About this same time, the church's board of elders asked my father to step up as the full-time head pastor after the previous pastor suddenly quit. The recession-ravaged economy of the early 1980s had already ended my father's small business. Now this congregation of about 200 people became the sole source of income for our family, and it wasn't enough. I watched my parents struggle to pay the bills.

Sometimes a member of the congregation would bring over a bag of groceries for us. Once my father discovered an envelope of cash in his coat pocket, placed there by an anonymous benefactor. The church could be giving and kind one day, but quick to judge the next.

If a wayward son guilty of vandalism had forced the resignation of an elder, I could scarcely imagine what the church would do to the head pastor if his son slipped into more serious sin. That would bring shame, tears, and financial ruin to the family, I thought. At this moment, I decided never to cause trouble for my father or my family. But with the stakes so high, merely staying out of trouble would not be good enough. I needed to do more. I would become the ideal Christian boy.

Following the Bible is a good start to become the ideal Christian boy. I could have written an appendix: "The Ideal Christian Boy in the American Evangelical Church." By the time I was a junior in high school, parents told me they hoped their sons would grow up to be like me. And why not? I was a saint. I led Bible studies. I sang in the choir. I traveled on short-term mission trips, visiting some of the poorest neighborhoods in Mexico. I committed large passages of the Bible to memory. At sixteen, an age when most boys have girls and other fascinating things on their minds, I memorized the entire Biblical book of Proverbs and recited each chapter with fewer than three errors. It took me most of the school year to do it. I also memorized the book of Philippians, the Sermon on the Mount, and many of the Psalms. I became a teenage encyclopedia of Biblical knowledge.

Preaching was the next logical step. At age seventeen, I wrote my first sermon as part of a project in my conservative Baptist school. It was titled "One Little Nail" because the sermon was based on the story of a man who let a problem with a simple nail eventually ruin his house. The sermon drove home the point that all it takes is one little sin and your life could be ruined.

After practicing the sermon at school several times, our principal asked me to deliver it at a mid-week service to the church congregation that had now grown to several hundred. When the time came, I strode to the front of the church and placed my Bible on the plain wooden pulpit. A six-foot wooden cross was on the wall behind me, scripture banners made of felt hanging on either side. By that age, I was already more than six feet tall, on my way up to six-four and more than two hundred pounds. A big guy—everyone could see me clearly. I opened the sermon without preamble or rambling introduction and launched right into it.

Speaking in front of the crowd was an isolating yet powerful experience for me. In individual conversations, I came across as shy and quiet at best, aloof and detached at worst. When face-to-face with someone, I fretted over every nonverbal cue or facial expression, second-guessing myself and stumbling over my words. But on the stage, I felt powerful and eloquent. I scanned the audience but didn't see individuals, just a blur of generic faces. With nobody directly interacting with me, my thoughts came out orderly and succinctly.

From the comfortable isolation of the stage, I got my first taste of what I could really do, and the impact of my intellect and the power of my words. The experience filled me with a boldness I would otherwise not have. This became the start of a speaking career that put me in front of thousands of people over the years and marked my life with a kind of irony—forceful, dynamic, and inspiring in front of thousands, but shy and clumsy in front of a single person.

This must have been an amusing sight for the congregation: a lanky teenager with a Bible in one hand, the other hand making sweeping gestures over the assembly, and a booming voice with the cadence of an old-time revival preacher. For that one service, I gazed down upon a congregation listening in rapt attention. This was the same congregation whose judgment I had feared as a ten-year old boy. Now they were listening to me preach. When I was done, I took a seat nonchalantly amid the applause: triumphant, set apart, untouchable.

Later, many people would ask, "When will you go into the ministry?" The church was beginning to have visions of a Billy Graham-like dynasty, with the ministry being handed down from father to son. This same congregation that judged Gary and his father, now regarded me with admiration and pride.

I began to believe my own hype. I knew I was good.

Of course, you want your sons to grow up to be like me.

From my lofty vantage point, it was easy to judge others. When other young people in my church faltered, I wondered how they could be so foolish. A student left our church school for the public schools because he could not adhere to our strict rules. I was convinced it was a simple failure of moral willpower and self-discipline. A teenage girl I knew became pregnant. How could she have let that happen? The Bible is very plain on this subject: we must abstain from sex until we are married. I looked at this girl and her swelling belly and wondered how she could fail to adhere to what seemed to me to be a very simple commandment.

As the 1980s came to a close, everything was simple and easy for me—black and white. Instead of being fearful of judgment, I became an expert at it. It was easy to be an expert when nothing had challenged my worldview.

four

A Word of Knowledge

In December of 2008, I arrived home from work—the last day of work before the holidays—and went out to retrieve the mail. Mixed in with the catalogs and coupons was a pale blue envelope with the words SUMMONS FOR JUROR SERVICE. I tore off the perforated edges and slid it open. There was nothing in the summons but logistical details, such as where and when I was to appear. Still, something happened to me at that moment. A series of pictures began to appear in my mind, as if I was staring at a screen in front of me. The pictures moved from one to the next like a slideshow.

A courtroom full of people.

A cluster of reporters with notebooks coming toward me with outstretched microphones.

A woman crying and seated at a large table.

I stood at the kitchen counter for what must have been several minutes watching this mental slideshow before the garage door opened. My wife, Molly, and our kids arrived home.

"Hey," Molly said, as she came into the kitchen.

The garage door slammed, and the kids (age eight and five) dropped their backpacks and ran upstairs. I was startled by their arrival. I was still standing in the kitchen holding the jury notice but had no idea how long I had been there.

She looked at the pale blue postcard. "Uh oh," she said with a smile. "You got jury duty!"

"Yeah," I replied, not matching her humorous tone.

"When?"

"February 11."

"Well, at least it isn't on your birthday."

"No, but I'm not going to get out of it this time."

I had received these pale blue letters before, only to call the jury hotline the night before and listen to the message that dismissed me from service without even going to the courthouse. This time, it was going to be different—I knew it.

Right there in our kitchen, I told my wife, "This is going to be a big, serious case with a lot of news coverage. I'm going to be chosen as the foreperson. And there's going to be a woman who I'm going to have to talk off the ledge. She is going to be crying that she can't do this. I'm going to have to figure out a way to get the group to a verdict. And I'll be blamed if we don't."

In the time I had stood by myself in the kitchen, I had seen all of this. But my wife didn't seem that impressed. She was more concerned about schedules, how we would manage our busy lives with the inflexibility of jury duty, and if I would still be paid if there was an absence from work.

"I guess we'll figure all that out when it happens," she said, "if you end up on the jury at all."

I didn't tell my wife how vivid my vision was—how I saw the

woman crying, sitting on the edge of a chair, her head down on a table, cradled inside her elbow. Her blond hair spilled over her arm onto the table as her shoulders rose and fell with her sobs. This vision left me depressed and anxious at the same time. I tucked the light blue postcard into the stack of bills with other items I would deal with later. Maybe I could just forget about this during the holidays, I thought to myself.

◆ ◆ ◆

In the church I attended growing up, my kitchen-counter vision would have been called a "word of knowledge," which is considered a message from God, similar to a prophecy. My childhood church was a charismatic church, and we believed in the gifts of the Holy Spirit: charismatic, supernatural gifts including healing, prophecy, and speaking in tongues. It was not unusual for our worship services to feature one or more of these supernatural gifts for the entire congregation to witness. Anyone who felt the calling of the Holy Spirit could stand in front of the congregation with a microphone and go where the spirit led.

For example, a person with a word of knowledge might tell the congregation: "There is someone here today who is worried about finances, and God wants you to know that He will provide for you."

Sometimes the word of knowledge would be very specific: "A woman here today is harboring a lot of anger toward her father and hasn't spoken to him for many years. God wants you to reconcile. Come up to the front right now, so we can pray you will have the strength to forgive."

Nearly every time someone would respond to the word of knowledge. The response might come after a long, awkward silence, but someone would eventually come to the front. The congregation would then pray for this person and offer words of encouragement. If you attended a mainstream, non-charismatic church, you would likely find this strange, suspicious, or even spooky. But we regarded this as evidence that God directly intervened in the everyday lives of His people.

Almost anything reasonable could be said in a word of knowledge, and it would usually apply to someone in the congregation. Speaking in tongues was much more bizarre and much bolder. Someone who felt the "urging of the Holy Spirit" stood at the microphone and talked for a minute or so in a language nobody on the planet could recognize. It sounded like babbling, but we believed it was actually the voice of the Holy Spirit. Helpfully, the Holy Spirit would provide another person in the congregation with an interpretation. That person would follow the tongues-speaker to the microphone and tell us all, in English, what was just said. Usually the message was about the glory of God, or an admonishment to live a holy life. And who could argue? It wasn't like we understood the nouns, adjectives, and verb conjugations of the spirit language.

Growing up with all this, I learned to view the spirit gifts—the words of knowledge, tongues, and even people claiming to be healed of various ailments—as quite normal. With these memories refreshed in my mind, I reflected on my kitchen counter vision. The vision reminded me of a word of knowledge. I tried to explain it away, telling myself that it was natural for the mind to wander and imagine the biggest possible outcomes. Someone who had just received a jury summons would naturally imagine it was for a big case with media coverage and jurors breaking down in difficult deliberations. Perhaps I had seen too many courtroom dramas on television, and this fueled my imagination. Whatever happened, I couldn't deny that the vision was vivid and detailed. Nothing like it had ever happened to me before, even during the hundreds of charismatic, spirit-filled church services I attended growing up.

The realness of the vision forced me to confront something in my life I'd been working to put behind me. I didn't want a word of knowledge to be true. I didn't believe in words of knowledge anymore. Or tongues. Or even the value of prayer. To believe in these things meant I had to believe that God's spirit was intervening in my life, in real-time. That God was right beside me, listening to me, and me to Him. In the evangelical vernacular, this was called "walking with the Lord." I hadn't been walking with the Lord lately, praying, or doing anything else with Him. Frankly, I felt betrayed by God, and I was angry.

five

THE CAUSE OF GOD

It should come as no surprise that I met my wife, Molly, at church. I noticed the new girl in attendance at the young adult Sunday School class, a group of single adults right out of the college years. She was about five and a half feet tall, with short and stylish reddish-brown hair and a broad smile with perfect teeth. A classic beauty, with high cheekbones and a slender chin. She was attractive. Pretty. I would have even said sexy, but I was in church and I was teaching the lesson that day.

It wasn't until a get-together at a friend's house later that afternoon that I spoke to her. There were no chairs left in the house where we were having lunch, so I sat on the floor, my back against a wall. Molly sat cross-legged on the floor across from me, just a few feet away. Molly was my opposite in so many ways. She engaged easily in conversation with anyone. I bravely made some small talk, but I sat there mostly silent, watching as she talked with others, smiling broadly and tossing her head back in laughter. Molly dressed that day plainly in shorts and a T-shirt with the logo of the Vanderbilt Baptist Student Union. I couldn't tell if she wore any makeup, and she wore no jewelry. I still found her beautiful without any of that, with a radiance that came from within. It wasn't the last time I would find myself gazing at her over the next few months. "Does she even realize how beautiful she is?" was a question I would ask myself many times.

I heard some bad news as she chatted with the others gathered around her. She mentioned something about a boyfriend—a long-distance relationship with a medical student back east. Of course, I thought to myself, a woman like that would already have a boy-friend—a doctor, no less.

At another church get-together a few weeks later, a glimmer of hope broke through the clouds.

"I can't believe this," Molly said to a couple ladies gathered around her. "My boyfriend sent me a sweatshirt for my birthday. A sweatshirt! Here we are hundreds of miles apart and he *knows* birthdays are a big deal to me. What does he do? Sends me a sweatshirt that he probably picked up at the university bookstore."

I had no business thinking I could attract a beautiful woman away from her aspiring doctor boyfriend. I had no dating experience and was terribly introverted when away from the safety of the stage or pulpit. Yet I couldn't help thinking that I had an opportunity. *That guy, whoever he is, will regret buying that sweatshirt.* Sometimes it is better to be lucky than good, and fortune was about to fall my way.

Even decades later, Molly and I still debate the date of our first date. I say it was January of 1995. Some of us in our church group decided to go skiing at Copper Mountain Resort, a ninety-minute drive from Denver. We were to meet early in the morning and carpool up to the mountain. The weather turned out to be gray and cold, with wind kicking up the snow. This type of weather would deter all but the most committed skiers. Sure enough, the phone calls came in from people deciding to skip the trip. The only one who still wanted to go was Molly. And so, the two of us set off. I had my chance at last.

We had plenty of time to talk, and as the day went on, I came out of my shell. We laughed and joked on the chairlift, seeing how long we could carry on a conversation in which every sentence ended in a rhyme. She attracted a lot of attention from other skiers because she was wearing a large hat that looked like a dog. The dog's ears covered her own ears, and the dog's nose was on her forehead.

"Cool hat," people told her.

"I know," she said, laughing. "It *is* awesome."

It took all my energy to keep up with Molly's outgoing personality and fun outlook on life. She was a better skier, too. A better driver, though, perhaps not so much.

Because we took her car, a red Toyota 4Runner, she drove. We made our way down the mountain on a snow-packed highway, with more snow swirling in the fading light. Molly chatted merrily along, taking her hand off the wheel to gesture. The car slipped a bit, and I tensed up. She laughed.

"Oooh, is my driving making you nervous?"

"Oh, no, not…really." I flattened myself against the seat back.

"I think I'm a pretty good driver in the mountains, even for a girl—don't you think?"

"Uh, I guess if I had to make a list of all the women I would trust driving in the mountains, I suppose you *could* be on that list." I didn't realize she had not engaged four-wheel drive.

Just a mile later, the road conditions deteriorated even more on a treacherously slippery snowpack. Molly needed to slow down, so she tapped on the brakes. Suddenly, the car spun around. We were backwards, facing the traffic behind us—and we continued to spin.

Molly yelled. "What do I do?! What do I do?!"

"Steer right—into the skid. Now left. Downshift." I was loud but surprisingly calm. I walked her through the process of steering out of a spin, as though I was reading from the definitive text on the subject. She sat bolt upright, too startled to yell.

Despite our efforts, we couldn't stop the slide. We rotated once more through a full spin while guardrails, signs, and other cars flashed briefly in the windshield like a slide show of winter road hazards. We seemed to be in slow motion. I noticed that the snow had been piled high in the median, probably three feet deep.

We are going to hit that snowdrift sideways, then we are going to roll over the drift and into the opposite lane where we will be hit by a truck.

We indeed smashed into the snow bank sideways, but the vehicle shuddered to a stop just a few paces away from a sign warning of sharp curves ahead. We hit nothing but snow, safely arriving in the median of the highway, perfectly between four lanes of afternoon ski traffic.

We sat there for a moment, flopped back against the seats, and listened to our hearts pounding. After a silence of a few seconds, Molly looked at me plaintively and said, "So, can I still get on that list?"

It was at that moment that I knew I needed this woman. I needed her fun and winsome personality and her love of impromptu adventure to balance out my seriousness and introversion.

"I'm sorry, but you are off the list," I replied with a smile.

"Good, because I'm shaking too much to drive."

I had once decided to become the ideal Christian boy. I now decided to be the ideal Christian boyfriend. I did everything right. I was thoughtful, creative, and generous. I drew beautiful notes and left them for her to find in places she would be throughout the day. I planned our dates down to the last detail. I lavished her with attention. To our friends at church, we exemplified the ideal couple, an example of how Christian dating should work. I wanted it no other way. Molly and I did everything but have sex, and that is because the teachings of the church forbade it. Chastity until marriage was a cause I had championed since my high school days.

◆ ◆ ◆

Preventing premarital sex was a big deal in my church-run school, resulting in plenty of preaching and teaching about it. Specific rules were enforced about how boys and girls were to behave. It wasn't enough simply to have a policy of no dating. Girls and boys could not even touch each other. In fact, the "six-inch rule" ensured that a holy half-foot was kept between the genders. Girls could not wear shorts or pants—their skirts must be long enough for the hem to touch the floor when kneeling in prayer.

With such a strict dress code, there was no way we could have a school swim team. Swimsuits are required for swimming, and swimsuits do not hide the curves of the female body. The curves of the female body were not helpful to fundamentalist boys. For us boys, we learned to keep any thoughts of girls out of our minds, for all sexual sin starts out as "the lust of the flesh." If we so much as looked at a woman with lust, we had "already committed adultery with her in your heart" (Matthew 5:28). The Bible continues, "If your right eye makes you stumble, tear it out and throw it from you; for it is better for you to lose one of the parts of your body, than for your whole body to be thrown into Hell." It says the same thing about your right hand. Better to cut that off, too, then to lose your whole body to the fires of Hell.

Being a fundamentalist Christian teenage boy, and especially the ideal Christian boy, was not an easy task. My life was full of contradictory signals. My body was telling me one thing, but the Bible, the preaching of the church, and the teachings of evangelical leaders like Dr. James Dobson were urging me in a different direction.

During the late 1980s and early 1990s, news of the AIDS crisis was everywhere. Conservative churches across America began to see sexual purity not only as a mandate of the Bible, but as an urgent health issue. It was of paramount importance to teach the youth of

America how to avoid the many perils of sex, and so that is what I did. And of course, the best way—God's way—to avoid AIDS or teen pregnancy or any other problem was through abstinence until marriage and monogamy thereafter.

In 1989, my church youth group teamed up with a Catholic youth group to travel around Colorado and speak to teenagers about the dangers of sex and the blessings of abstinence. I played a lead role in the speeches and skits. Traveling with me was Amy, a high school classmate of mine.

Amy was everything I was not. While I was cautious, conservative, and all-business, Amy was fun and bold. Once she grabbed my hand and pulled me toward something she wanted me to see, and I was suddenly like a puppy on a leash. She wantonly violated the six-inch rule, and had no problem giving me a playful punch on the shoulder or taking my arm and pulling me closer to her, leaving me frightened and thrilled all at once. Amy's attractiveness could not be hidden even in our drab, blue and gray school uniforms. I would sit behind her in chapel and watch mesmerized as she would pull her curly tangle of brown hair into a ponytail, revealing the nape of her neck.

I'm in God's holy church, I had to remind myself, hardening my discipline.

Amy and I went with our wandering band of abstinence minstrels on a trip to Alamosa, Colorado to speak to a high school group. She and I were to play the lead role in skit that would show everyone just how easy it is to say no to sex. Up on the stage, we placed a park bench, and the skit began with the two of us sitting side by side and talking about how much we liked each other. We inched closer together and then leaned in for a kiss. The adult leader of our group feared that two teenagers in a skit about abstinence might somehow, ironically, become aroused beyond control, so she told Amy to put her hand on her mouth, so our lips wouldn't touch. With her back to the audience, it looked like we were really kissing.

Secretly, I wanted more. I had denied myself a real kiss in the interest of following the rules and keeping myself pure for the cause of Christ. There I was in front of a small-town audience of sullen teenagers forced to assemble against their will to hear an abstinence talk. This stage kiss was the closest I ever came to kissing a girl until I was twenty-five years old.

◆ ◆ ◆

Despite my public zeal for sexual purity, or perhaps because of it, I began to catch the eye of more than a few girls in college. One in particular, Jennifer, had taken an interest in me. Jennifer was petite with radiant skin and blond, curly hair that gently brushed the tops of her shoulders.

In the summer of 1990, Jennifer took the same summer school speech class I was attending. Jennifer and I, plus two others, were put into a group for an assignment. We were supposed to present a critique of a product (we would get to pick one). Because it was summer school, none of us were in the mood for anything too serious, so we decided to critique a movie. When we all arrived at the theater to see *Days of Thunder*, Jennifer waited until I had chosen a seat before she nestled into the seat next to me.

I had dutifully brought a small notebook to record any notes we might need, straining to see it in the dark. I pretended not to notice when Jennifer leaned closer to me, our arms and shoulders touching. Or when she crossed her legs, and the toe of her sandal touched the back of my leg. Or when she leaned over to whisper something to me, placing her hand gently on my knee.

Meanwhile, there was a movie going on that I was supposed to be watching. It was about racecar drivers. Or something. There was a real, live girl sitting next to me. She *wanted* to sit next to me. Her touch was warm and soft. She smelled like summer, a mix of flowers and suntan lotion.

When our assignment was over, Jennifer asked if I would like to go out with her and some friends. I politely declined, hurriedly making up some excuse. I had never done anything before like "hanging out" with girls. Plus, I reasoned, they would probably want to drink, and alcohol was the second worst thing I could be doing.

I shouldn't have been worried about Jennifer. She was as wholesome as they come, raised in a small farm town in northeastern Colorado. Still, rules were rules. It never occurred to me that maybe I could spend time with a girl and not get drunk or have sex. I was focused on the teaching of the Bible: all sexual sin starts out with the "lust of the flesh," and even so much as "looking on a woman with lust in your heart" is just as bad as adultery. It was best, I thought, to avoid even the hint of temptation.

Amazingly, Jennifer didn't give up. Over the weeks that followed, she invited me to various activities. I always had an excuse to say no. When our class ended, I figured that I would not see her again and was surprised when Jennifer showed up at the computer store where I worked. I stood at the front of the store, behind the glass cabinet that held printer ribbons, floppy disks, and surge protectors. Because there were no customers, we were alone.

"I was thinking about you today," she said placing her hands on the edge of the glass cabinet. I noticed she was wearing a low-cut blouse. I forced my eyes up to meet hers.

We made the usual small talk discussing how the summer was going. As she talked, I focused on her blond hair bobbing up and down in tight curls, willfully resisting another look down at the blouse. Not knowing what else to do in front of a girl by myself, I pretended to continue working, kneeling to rearrange boxes of disks and printer ribbons in the cabinet while she talked on about her plans for the next semester of classes.

She leaned over the cabinet further, stretching to look down at me. "Let's go out," she said suddenly, "when you are off work. How about dinner?"

I pulled myself up to both feet and straightened my posture.

Damn the rules and go out with her.

I heard the fluorescent lights buzzing overhead as she waited for a reply. "Well, um, see, here's the thing," I finally said, my throat going dry. "I won't date until I'm ready to get married." I felt light-headed and my words seemed to echo inside my head. "And I want to date and then marry a Christian girl."

I looked up to see Jennifer straighten her posture. Her eyes widened, and her mouth dropped open. *I don't even know if she is a Christian,* I realized suddenly.

I didn't get a chance to say anything else. Jennifer turned aside as a hot shade of crimson washed over her face. There was a moment of silence before she turned and half-ran half-walked out the door and onto the sidewalk along College Avenue, her blond hair swaying side to side. That was the last time I saw Jennifer.

I turned at the counter to see two of my coworkers staring at me from around a corner, their mouths open in astonishment.

"Did you *see* her?" one of them asked incredulously. "Wow—she is a really pretty girl! What do you think you are doing?"

I looked down and saw I clutched a sliver box of 3M brand computer disks tightly in my hand.

Let them be astonished, I thought. I know what I'm doing is right. I know that God will reward me one day.

He *had* to reward me. God owed it to me. I had done everything He had asked, everything that was written in the Holy Bible, and everything taught by his disciples, from Dr. James Dobson on down.

If I had been called to a death penalty jury at that time of my life, it would have been an easy task. I was an excellent judge and an expert on sin, righteousness, and what God wanted from all of us. There would have been no agonizing over a death penalty decision. There would have been no moments when I wanted to yell in my car, trying to release the anxiety of an impossible choice between justice and mercy.

six

CHAIR TWELVE

I arrived for jury duty on February 11, 2009 at the Arapahoe County Courthouse. I cleared security and sat in a large room with about two hundred other potential jurors. Three men entered the room and one of them was introduced as Judge Gerald Rafferty. The judge read a statement thanking us for our service and describing how the jury selection process would work. He warned us that the trial would receive media coverage and that we were not to discuss it at all, nor follow any media coverage of the case. He told us that the trial would last ten weeks. Then he read this brief description of what the jury would consider:

> Sir Mario Owens ("Sir" is his actual first name), Robert Ray, and Perish Carter have been charged with the murders of Javad Marshall Fields and his fiancée, Vivian Wolfe, both of whom had recently graduated from Colorado State University. Mr.

Fields and Ms. Wolfe were shot in their vehicle at the intersection of South Dayton Street and East Idaho Place in Aurora, Colorado, on June 20, 2005. When he was shot, Mr. Fields was scheduled to testify as a witness the following week in the trial of Robert Ray for Accessory to Murder. Mr. Ray's trial concerned the shooting death of Gregory Vann and the wounding of Javad Fields and Elvin Bell at Lowry Park on July 4, 2004. The prosecution is seeking the death penalty against Robert Ray. Robert Ray has pleaded not guilty.

The judge further explained that Sir Owens and Perish Carter would be tried separately. The jury would only consider the case of Robert Ray, and if they found him guilty of first-degree murder, they would also have to decide his fate: life imprisonment without the possibility of parole or death by lethal injection.

We then answered a multi-page questionnaire that asked about our backgrounds, how much we already knew about this case, and our beliefs about the death penalty. If the attorneys liked what we wrote, they would call us back for phase two of the process: individual interviews with the judge and the attorneys. If we made it past that, there was a third phase of jury selection, the standard *voir dire* done in a group as in any other criminal case.

Mathematically speaking, the chances of being chosen for the jury were slim. They had called two thousand people over many days and were looking to narrow it down to twenty: twelve jurors and eight alternates. Even so, I went back to work and immediately looked up my employer's policy on jury duty, wondering what would happen if I had to take a long leave of absence. I learned one thing right away—my boss wasn't going to like it if I was called. He even emailed me a link to an article he found, "How to get out of jury duty. Five excuses that really work."

About two weeks later, I was called by the jury commissioner. She explained that I was to come back for the second phase of jury selection, an individual interview. Apparently, the answers I wrote in the questionnaire were satisfactory to the attorneys.

When I arrived for my interview, a bailiff led me to courtroom 401. He gave me a red, white, and blue sticker that said "JUROR" and told me to put it on my shirt. People in the hallways glanced at the patriotic JUROR sticker and then looked at me sympathetically, knowing I was there for the big trial. "You poor man," their expressions seemed to say.

Judge Rafferty was clad in a black robe and seated up high behind the bench. He instructed me to take a seat in the jury box, and I sat in the middle of all the empty chairs. I was the only potential juror there because this was an individual interview.

I glanced nervously around the room. The next person I noticed was a young black man seated at the defense table twenty feet in front of me. He was slender, clean-cut, and wearing a blue and green plaid button-down shirt. His hands were in his lap. We made eye contact for a split-second, and as soon as we did, he turned his gaze down to the table. We had not been formally introduced, but I figured I had just met the accused murderer, Robert Ray.

Sitting next to him were his attorneys. Across the aisle from them were two prosecuting attorneys. Three Sheriff's deputies were in the room as well, two guarding the main door and one guarding the back door of the courtroom.

One of the prosecutors walked over to the jury box and stood a few feet in front of me, dressed in a blue skirt, white blouse, and matching blazer. She seemed to be my age, maybe just a shade older. She smiled and introduced herself and her colleague and launched into her first question, "Why do you think we have the death penalty in Colorado?"

I paused for a couple seconds. "I believe the purpose of the death penalty is to punish especially heinous crimes. It's a statement that the state will only tolerate so much."

"A statement?" Her face showed surprise. "Is it a deterrent?"

"Apparently not," I said.

The prosecutor then spent several minutes going over a flow chart of the death penalty decision process mandated by the state. She knew I was in the software business, so she tried to explain it to me in computer programming terms. She presented it as if deciding to kill a man for his crimes was like writing an if-then statement in a software program. With this type of statement, given the right inputs, you must necessarily arrive at a programmed outcome. Then she asked directly if I could make this decision. If I thought Robert Ray was deserving of the death penalty, could I actually sentence him to death?

This is where the computer analogy broke down. Some things just don't fit neatly into the prosecutor's equation, like mercy. At the same time, justice is a necessary thing for society. I had just said that the death penalty was a statement that society would only tolerate so much. But would I be willing to sentence Robert Ray to death in order to make a *statement*? How could I balance the competing ideals of justice and mercy?

The prosecutor was waiting for my answer. I scanned the room nervously. I had to answer the question right in front of the accused? I asked her to repeat the question.

"If Robert Ray is guilty," she said slowly, gesturing back to Robert Ray without looking his way, "and you believe he deserves the death penalty, are you able to make that decision?" I looked down, so I wouldn't see Robert Ray.

"Yes."

"Thank you. I'm all done." She turned back toward her chair.

I looked away from Robert Ray because I didn't want to see his reaction. I had just said I believed the death penalty was sometimes necessary to show that society will only tolerate so much—we would draw a line. Now a defendant with a face and a name was sitting before me in business casual wardrobe that wouldn't look out of place at my own office. He was accused of crossing that line—my line.

Anxiety crept up from my gut into my throat, and it felt tight, sick, and hot. At that moment, I realized a crack had formed in my hard exterior. I had grown up living in a black and white world where sin was sin, and, as it says in the book of Romans, "The wages of sin is death." Yet, I had some thoughts and traits I hadn't known were there: mercy, mitigation, and the idea that there were situations more nuanced than what I had been taught. This moment in courtroom 401 was an amazing revelation to me. I was seeing shades of gray.

I didn't have a chance to ponder this for more than a few moments because it was time for questions from the defense team. One of the attorneys stood from his chair quickly and strode to the center of the room, his eyes narrowing under a furrowed brow, no smile on his face. He didn't offer any words of greeting or introduction. He launched straightaway into his questions.

"What will make you consider mercy for my client?" His voice was flat.

"What do you mean *make me*?" I was puzzled.

"What if he was really young when he committed the crime—would that help you?" He seemed annoyed that I didn't understand his question.

"I suppose that would be good to know. But it would depend on how young. I guess."

"What if he was exposed to a life of crime as a boy—would that help you?"

His tone surprised me. I felt like he was angry at me. He didn't look me in the eye.

"Are you asking if I will take his background into consideration?" I asked him.

"What if his parents did a bad job raising him?" He apparently ignored my question. "Or what if his brothers were a bad influence on him—would that help you?"

"Well, I would want to know his background. Is *that* what you mean?"

There were a few more questions like this before the judge interjected that there was only a minute left in the interview.

"Are you going to be a bully, Mr. Dubler?" The question came out quickly, forcefully.

"A bully?"

The attorney raised his voice and now he looked me in the eye for the first time. "Are you going to bully another juror who wants to give my client mercy?"

"Well, no, why would…"

"What if there is someone who wants to give him mercy?"

"Well, I…"

"What if there is one person—*one person*—who doesn't agree with everyone else? You are going to pressure that person to change their decision, aren't you? *Aren't you?*" Now he had moved to within arm's reach of me.

"No, absolutely not." I felt uncomfortable as he got closer to me with his voice raised. My face grew warm. I squared my shoulders in response, trying to be brave.

"Are you going to defend the person who wants to give my client mercy? Will you stand up for them and protect them from bullying by the other jurors?"

I didn't get a chance to answer that one. The judge interrupted and said time was up.

The attorney objected. "I'm not done here. Mr. Dubler hasn't answered my question." He looked right at me. There was a pause. I said nothing and looked toward the judge.

"This interview is over," the judge said.

"Judge, I object!"

"Noted, but overruled." Then motioning toward the back door, the judge told me to go back to the jury room and wait a few minutes for the attorneys' decision about me. The attorney scowled and stepped back toward his chair but kept his eyes on me as I headed for the door.

As I followed the bailiff out the door I thought I was going to dodge this bullet. With the way things had ended, the defense would clearly not want me on the jury. I imagined that in a few minutes I would be calling my wife, relieved to tell her the news. The door clicked shut behind us. Then, after I took only a few steps down the hall, the door opened again, and a deputy waved me back in to the jury box. "You may stay standing," the judge said. He looked down and read from a sheet of paper. "Juror 1296, you have *not* been excused and are instructed to return at 8:30 a.m. on Monday, April 6, 2009, for group questioning and final jury selection."

My throat went dry. I squeaked out a "Yes, sir," and headed for the door. I stole a quick glace back toward the attorneys. The defense attorney who questioned me was leaning back nonchalantly in his chair. Robert Ray stared straight ahead, his hands in his lap. One of the prosecutors was writing on a notepad, her head bent over the table. I learned after the trial that she showed it to her colleague. The note said, "That's the foreperson."

◆ ◆ ◆

On Monday, April 6, one month after my individual interview with the attorneys, I arrived at the courthouse with ninety-nine other potential jurors for one more round of jury selection. This time we were together in one group. We crowded into courtroom 201, sitting in numbered chairs. The attorneys were going to select twelve jurors and eight alternates. We were seated according to our likelihood of being selected. Those in chairs 1-20 were more likely to be on the jury than those in chairs 80-100. I was in chair thirty-three. For me to be on the jury, twelve people in chairs 1-20 would first have to be removed—*struck*—from the jury pool because the lawyers didn't like something about them.

Before the questions began, the judge introduced each attorney, and they stood so we could see them. Then the judge motioned toward the defendant and said, "And this is the defendant, Mr. Ray."

Robert Ray seemed taken aback by this, and he stood up awkwardly about halfway and raised his hand slightly in a sort of wave to the crowd. This seemed unnecessary. We all knew who this man was. How awkward it must have been for him to stand and wave to the people who would decide his fate. As I thought about it, I realized what the judge was doing. He was making a statement: this man was a defendant, not a convict. He was innocent until proven guilty. He was a citizen like everyone else in the room. He was a person, worthy of recognition.

When the questioning started, jurors seemed to adopt one of two strategies: be outspoken and a little eccentric, or keep quiet.

The first question was about making big decisions and was directed to a young lady seated near the front of the room. She said she panicked when asked to make big decisions and couldn't, in fact, make any decisions. She admitted that in her job she was afraid to make any decision without first consulting her manager. Nearly in tears she said, "I can't do anything unless I know my manager approves."

A man also seated near the front in a low-numbered chair was quick to raise his hand to answer any question. He gave rambling answers and ended each with, "Well, I probably answered too soon because I really don't know what I think. I'm just brainstorming out loud."

When asked if racism was a real factor in American life, one woman objected strenuously to the idea of even asking that question. "How dare you insinuate that I'm a racist," she said. "I don't consider the defendant to be black or white or anything. He is clear. That's right, I see no color at all."

An older man seated somewhere behind me dodged a question asked to him. Instead, he complained that the crowded room was unsafe. He pointed out that we had not been briefed on what to do in an emergency if we needed to evacuate the room. He suggested the jury selection was illegal since the room seemed crowded beyond the official fire marshal limits.

The questioning continued for about two hours, during which time I decided the best strategy was to lay low. I didn't volunteer to answer any questions, and I didn't jump in on the conversation. As a result, I was asked only one direct question: something to do with whether or not I would have trouble making a fair decision if the defense didn't call any witnesses.

When all the questioning was finally done, the attorneys began to strike people from the jury. The first to go was the woman afraid of making any decisions. Next was the man who wanted to answer every question, followed by the self-proclaimed color-blind woman. All the outspoken or eccentric ones were quickly dismissed. Perhaps they knew exactly what they were doing. Perhaps I had chosen the wrong strategy.

After about thirty minutes, twelve people had been ejected from the jury box, and I was next in line. The prosecution dismissed the person in chair twelve, and the judge ordered me to take her place. I left chair thirty-three, where I had been sitting quietly all day, and took my place in chair twelve. With that decision, jury selection was complete, and I would spend the next ten weeks as a juror in case 06CR697: People vs. Robert Ray.

The vision or word of knowledge or whatever it was I had experienced at my kitchen counter half a year before suddenly became quite real. As I stood to follow the bailiff to the jury room for further instructions, I had to steady myself, gripping the back of a chair. I was lightheaded from the shock. I couldn't tell myself any longer that I was a *potential* juror. This was the real deal. All the questions I had pondered during jury selection flooded my mind. Why was there a death penalty? What would make me consider mercy? Was I going to be a bully? If the death penalty was appropriate, could I go through with it? There was no way I could be ready for this. I wanted more time to think things over, but time was up. I had been chosen for the jury despite my background and struggles, and the hopeless contradictions the questioning raised in me.

seven

Useless Righteousness

Jury selection was over, and I walked trance-like out of the courthouse to the parking lot. I sat in my car for a few minutes, hoping the worry and dread would subside.

"I'm not happy with you, God," I said under my breath, "for a lot of things. If you are behind this, I sure hope you know what you are doing." I stopped myself, surprised again at what the jury selection process provoked in me. *Am I praying? Did I just talk to God?*

The reality was I had long ago stopped believing in words of knowledge, prophecies, speaking in tongues, or even the power of prayer. This was a remarkable turnaround from my youth as the ideal Christian boy, the one who in his zealousness would take the fight for God and righteousness to the public square. This wasn't a sudden change, but one that happened gradually as I was worn down by personal failures.

My wife had the best view of my disintegration of faith. When we were dating, Molly said the most appealing thing about me was that I was a committed Christian, and the most spiritual person she had ever met. Indeed, we prayed together often and engaged in long and deep conversations about God. In the Summer of 1996, when our wedding was 150 days away, we read Psalms chapter 150 together from the Bible. The next day we read chapter 149, and we kept at it each day, using the chapters as a countdown to our wedding. When business travel took me away, we got on the phone to read. Our courtship and wedding were bathed in prayer, structured by the holy scriptures, and full of positive promise. That is why what happened to us next came as a complete shock.

◆　◆　◆

"I want a companion." Molly was shouting. "You are just a room-mate." She waved her hand at me dismissively.

"Quiet, or you'll wake the girl!" I was referring to our toddler-age daughter, asleep upstairs while we sat in the living room.

Molly dropped onto our hunter-green leather couch. "So what? Do you want to hide our problems from her, too, and just live in denial that everything is okay?"

Molly doubled over in tears, her arms folded across her stomach. I sat on the matching loveseat a few feet away at a ninety-degree angle from the couch. After four years of living in our first home, a 1970 model two-story, we could finally afford some new furniture. The rest of the living room still resembled the disco era, with painted-over paneling, a dark rock fireplace and chimney, and a lamp that hung by a brass colored chain.

I moved over to the couch and sat next to Molly. I knew that this is what a husband should do for a crying wife. I put my arm on one of her shoulders in a halfway hug, but she didn't react to my touch. She just sat and sobbed, head down, her shoulders shuddering when she exhaled.

I stared out the glass patio door and into the night, completely out of ideas. These outbursts had happened before. It was true: I had distanced myself. It was easier than tackling our disappointments head-on. I would normally say almost anything to get the crying to end. But on that night, I just sat, one hand on her shoulder and waited.

"Oh God," she wailed, "this hurts too much."

Oh God, indeed, I said to myself. Is this the reward you promised for a chaste life devoted to you?

It is true that all marriages are a struggle at times, and many couples find themselves on the brink of divorce. It is also true that most marriages have a honeymoon period, a time of blissful satisfaction. At least those couples can look back during the difficult times and remember the honeymoon. Not us. We were cheated out of our honeymoon.

I didn't expect to be a legendary lover. After all, I was a twenty-six-year-old virgin when we married. I knew that we would have plenty of learning to do. But it would be happy work, a journey of delightful discovery. But this is not what happened, even in our beautiful honeymoon destination of Hawaii.

I was surprised with how awkward and difficult it was to have sex for the first time. I didn't expect to be as squeamish as I was about the mechanics and messiness. Perhaps it was our high expectations and great anticipation for blessed married life. Perhaps my innate perfectionism set me up to fail. Maybe the fatigue of a large wedding (nearly five hundred guests) and the travel immediately afterward compounded the problems. Whatever the reasons, we did not have a good wedding night, and this came as a shock to us.

In one night, everything I had hoped for, everything I strove to attain, vanished. Worse yet, the foundation of my faith—strive for righteousness and God will reward me—crumbled along with it. We tried to recover in Hawaii, but I could not get over the disappointment I felt. Then the anticipation was replaced by fear and doubt. We flew home to begin our life together and I couldn't help but think it was paradise lost.

Now, several years later, I watched helplessly as my wife cried. "Oh God," she wailed, "I am so lonely."

By then, the problems were about more than just sex. Confronted by disappointment and failure, I withdrew from any kind of intimacy—physical, emotional, or spiritual. We did manage sex on occasion (we did have two children), and there were some fun times as well. But the only area where I felt any success was in practical matters like finances, raising our two children, and managing the household. That was not enough for us. We expected bliss. We expected passion. We expected deep connection and longing. We expected a blessed marriage that would be better than most, or at least better than secular ones. Instead, we both felt abandoned. Molly felt abandoned by me, and I in turn felt abandoned by God.

While she might hide it for weeks or even months, Molly's emotional pain and disappointment in our marriage would always return, and each time it would boil over, I would be more unsure of what to do.

As we sat on the green leather couch that day, I tried to be helpful. "Lots of couples struggle worse than us," I said. "We actually have a lot of positives in our marriage."

"You just don't get it," she replied, a look of exasperation seizing her face. "Why are you like this? I am sick to death of you pretending like we don't have serious problems. This is not normal. You don't know what it is like to be completely abandoned by the one person who is supposed to want me more than anything. I can't take it. This hurts so much—I'd rather die."

I stared at the glass door and the reflection of the two of us sitting on the couch. *Can this really be happening?* The reflection showed the reality: an agonized wife doubled over in tears, and a dazed husband, shoulders slouched.

"You don't mean that." I pulled my hand from her shoulder. "I know I've got things to work on, but we are not in a bad marriage."

"You have no idea." Molly at last turned her head to face me in tears. "I don't even know if you are capable of understanding. I would have divorced you years ago, and the only reason I haven't is because I'm a Christian."

"Well praise the Lord!" I said sarcastically.

◆　◆　◆

Our marriage drifted into dysfunction, with long droughts of sexual and emotional intimacy. We filled up our lives with the busy work of two careers, two children, and all the activities that came with that. Even though we functioned well in practical matters, the hurt and disappointment was always the undercurrent that threatened to someday catch hold and sink us. Molly would often credit God for keeping her in our marriage. Once she told me that she prayed to God that one of us would die, it didn't matter which, so we could be rid of the pain. In later years, she tempered that by saying that God would simply have to help her be content with a husband that apparently couldn't be an intimate companion, sexual or otherwise.

These statements about God's role in our marriage hurt the most. Obedience to God was of paramount importance when I was young. I not only sacrificed my own desires, I made myself a public example of how a Christian young man should behave. The church taught clearly that sexual abstinence until marriage was honoring to God, and if we complied, God would "bless our sex lives" when we married. Sex was a beautiful gift from God to be opened only in marriage.

These statements were repeated so often from the pulpit of evangelical churches, it had become cliché. Yet I knew total heathens whose marriages were better than mine. As I would eventually learn, lots of people "lived in sin," risking the wrath of a holy God with plenty of ravenous sex before they were married, and yet they were happier in marriage than I was. This was in complete and bewildering defiance of all the preaching I had heard and even done myself. It says in the book of Proverbs, a Biblical book I memorized at age sixteen, "The rain falls on the righteous and the unrighteous." Still, I couldn't believe it. Nothing God or His church had promised came true for me. My life of righteousness felt like a complete waste.

One of the more popular stories in the Bible is the parable Jesus told of the prodigal son. The story is of a young man with a wealthy father. He decided not to wait for the formality of his father's death to get his inheritance. He asked for it in advance. Surprisingly, the father gave his son the money and the young man went off into the world. The son spent the money on a wild career of debauchery with all the food, wine, and women he could buy. At last his money ran out, and he was forced to live in poverty and near starvation, stealing the food he was supposed to be feeding to pigs in the only job he could find.

One day the prodigal son realized he would be better off as a servant in his father's house than eating pig food and living in squalor. He set out determined to beg forgiveness, grovel at his father's feet, and take any menial job his father would give him. Instead, his father gave him a new robe, a gold ring, and re-established him as his son and heir of his estate. He then held a magnificent feast to celebrate. It went on for days.

The story is supposed to give hope to sinners who have spurned their Heavenly Father. If they only seek forgiveness, God will raise them up again, even those who squandered their lives on atrocious sin. Most people who know the story have only heard it up to this point, and don't realize the story has a very odd and disconcerting ending.

While the feast was going on, the prodigal's accomplished and righteous elder brother returned from his usual hard day of work in the field. He was shocked to see his little brother back home and became indignant at the extravagant celebration.

"I've devoted my life to you without fail," he said to his father. "And yet you have never even thrown a small party for me. Now here comes my loser brother after he blew his inheritance on prostitutes, and you set him up like royalty."

The father tells the elder brother he shouldn't feel this way, and he should be glad that his little brother, whom they thought was dead, was back now with the family. That's it. End of story. No further explanation. No comfort for the elder brother. No recognition for his life of righteous behavior and hard work.

I heard this story dozens of times in my life. But the part about the elder brother was just a footnote, until I found myself sleeping alone in our bedroom. Molly, acting out of frustration, tried many things to get through to me. One night, as she gathered up her pillows, she informed me she would be sleeping in the guest room.

"Maybe you'll realize what I am feeling now." She pulled a blanket out from under my legs and walked to the door. She wasn't angry. She was eerily calm, and that's what scared me.

"What? Molly, this is ridiculous. You can't manipulate me with a stunt like this!"

She turned around, her eyes confident. She shrugged, unconcerned how I viewed this. "I'm not divorcing you, and this is not a separation." She stared at me, over the top of the pillows clutched to her chest. "But it's as close as I can get right now. I need it. Maybe you'll see what that would be like."

"Can't we just talk about this?" I felt a tightness in my chest. I strained my neck to see as she walked out the door.

"Good night." She disappeared down the hallway.

"What standards do I have to meet before you'll come back?" I thought this was a valid point, that her plan lacked any clear goals, and she would soon see the silliness of it all.

"You don't get it."

The door to the guest room closed, and I sat alone on our bed.

For several nights, I laid awake and alone in our bedroom, staring into the dark. I wondered if I should go join Molly in the guest room, to show her that I was going to take action. Each time that thought crept in, anxiety seemed to keep me pinned to the bed—the tightness in my chest. The tightness would give way to heaviness, depression, shame. If it was possible to wear a dunce cap in bed, I would have worn one.

As I lay alone in bed on one of those nights, a thought flashed into my mind: I was the elder brother. Maybe it would have been better to have sex a few times before marriage, to "go prodigal" for a while. God apparently was in a forgiving mood for prodigals, and maybe even enjoyed having them come home. Maybe it gave Him a sense of purpose. Maybe God needed an excuse to party. I wondered what God considered worse: a bit of fornication or a dysfunctional marriage?

After a few nights, Molly returned to our bed, not because she felt victorious or saw some change in me. She just didn't sleep well on the firmer mattress in the guest bedroom. We returned to our regular dysfunction together in the same bed, and I settled into a depression brought on by the realization that I had lived a life of useless righteousness. I wished I was the prodigal: imperfect but celebrated. Nobody celebrates the righteous older brother. His accomplishments and constancy are boring.

As the years went by, I drifted further and further away from God. I still believed in God, but now I regarded Him as a distant power who set the world in motion but didn't bother to interact with His creation. He did miracles in the past, but not any longer. He certainly did not care to intervene in my life. I still went to church with Molly, and I put on a good face for it, mainly for our kids. I would sit in His church and be polite, but I didn't interact. I didn't pray. God didn't need me or my testimony of righteous living, so I saw no reason why He should get my tithe money, a full ten percent of my income, to pay for the work of His church.

As the opening day of the trial approached, I wondered which version of me would show up—the righteous, legalistic one who saw the world in black and white, or the one humbled and broken by his personal failures? Would the suburban dad who had experienced crime only from news reports and episodes of *Law & Order* be able to comprehend a world of drugs, gangs, and murder? The fate of one man and the expectations of an entire community depended on the answers.

eight

SACRIFICE

The door to the courtroom swung open with a slight squeak. "All rise!" said a male voice from just inside the door, out of view.

I filed in past a Sheriff's deputy who was holding the door. I was twelfth in a line of twenty jurors, entering through the back door of the courtroom, facing the crowd in the gallery. I saw dozens of people standing up from their chairs, setting notebooks and purses on the floor as they straightened up. The seats of each chair flipped up like they do in movie theaters, folding up with a creak and a *thunk*. I caught a brief glimpse of the defendant standing behind the defense table, with his hands together at the waist, his face expressionless. Another deputy stood behind him, leaning against the wall, his belt heavy with a gun on one side, a Taser on the other. Two more deputies stood at each side of the main door to the courtroom, where those in the gallery came and went.

Judge Rafferty told us earlier that in *his* courtroom, everyone stands when the jury enters or exits, including him. It was a sign of respect, he said, for our position and the personal sacrifice it took to serve in a trial of this magnitude. I didn't like this protocol, this drawing of attention to me. I didn't want any statements or reminders of my new importance to the community—as someone who would judge the deeds of a man, and if guilty, sentence him to a life in prison or death row. I lowered myself into chair twelve, leaning on both armrests heavily.

The judge stood beside his chair, black robe covering his wiry frame. Just thirty minutes earlier, he stopped by our cramped jury room with a box of donuts. "I'm here to ruin your diet," he said with a smile. "But only for this week, since you are all new here. You're on your own next week."

With a cardigan sweater over his shirt and tie, and thin, gray hair, he looked like a grandfather surprising his grandchildren with donuts. I imagined him standing at the cashier with the box of donuts, carefully counting out exact change from a coin purse, like my own grandfather used to do.

The grandfatherly demeanor belied the judge's own history. We were talking about him during a break when one of the bailiffs mentioned that our donut-bearing judge was once an Air Force fighter pilot and an FBI special agent. From up on the bench, he commanded the room with a stern gaze.

"You may be seated," the judge said.

We jurors all sat down. I heard the dull clattering of notebooks opening and the creak of swivel chairs in the jury box. Then the judge said the words we would hear every time we came back into the courtroom, "Case 06CR697, people versus Robert Ray, is now in session. The jury is present, as is Mr. Ray."

The bailiff had given each juror a large notebook, and I opened mine to the first page. It was blank and crisp, with college-ruled lines in a faint blue. I wrote "06CR697" in the top right corner, as if I might forget what this notebook was all about. I then wrote "April 8" on the top line. It was Wednesday morning, April 8, 2009. Six months had elapsed since I received that pale blue postcard in my mailbox, but I still didn't feel ready.

I can't believe this is happening.

I wanted more time to prepare like I would for a business meeting, anticipating questions and researching the answers. I had no such luxury now, no time to contemplate or prepare my mind. Ready or not, we were underway.

◆　◆　◆

Hollywood courtroom dramas are always set in beautiful old courthouses, with grand lobbies at the top of stone steps, high ceilings, and marble floors. The light from tall windows reflects on warm mahogany-paneled walls, bathing the scene in rich gold and brown hues. When I arrived at my courthouse the first day of trial, I laughed, recalling the Hollywood image. The Arapahoe County courthouse is a blocky, red-brick structure banded by narrow windows, the roofline cluttered with vents, air conditioners, and antennas. Inside, the carpet is worn, the walls a faint white, and the doors scuffed from being kicked open countless times by lawyers struggling with large boxes of papers. Fluorescent lamps, often of slightly different shades of white, lit the rooms with the same warmth as a warehouse.

The courthouse felt more like an airport, with lines of people snaking through the crowded lobby, waiting their turn to walk through the security scanners. A guard noticed my juror badge and waved me to the front.

"Excuse me, excuse me," I repeated as I edged my way through the lines of people who stepped aside with no eye contact. At least at an airport, people look forward to their destinations, which helps them endure the indignities of modern travel. In this concourse of crime and punishment, each downcast face and weary sigh extinguished any hope of joy. Only tragedies and evil brought one to this place.

I took off my belt, removed keys and wallet from my pockets, and sent them down the X-ray conveyor. Ahead of me in line was Kelly, another juror. I recognized her from the last day of jury selection. Kelly stepped through the metal detector. Despite no audible alarm from the metal detector, the guard motioned her aside for another scan using a hand-held wand. Kelly was a former college soccer star, young and attractive. The guard took his time passing the wand up each of her legs and over the small of her back. The wand chirped as he ran it carefully over her chest.

When the guard was finally done with his careful examination of Kelly, he waved me through. I took a step through the scanner and looked up at him.

"You're good to go," he said. "Have a nice day."

We would laugh about this often in the jury room, as Kelly was usually one of the last to arrive, always delayed by the wand scan.

"I don't know," she said laughing about it one morning, "there must be something about me."

Indeed. What I noticed about Kelly was her straight, blond hair that flowed smoothly over her shoulders, just like the woman in my vision six months before I met any of the jurors. I had never seen the face of my vision, just her blond hair spilling over her arm and onto a table as she had cradled her head in the crook of her elbow, her shoulders rising and falling with her sobbing. I tried to reason with myself about this vision.

You heard a story somewhere of a juror breaking down during a difficult trial and you simply pictured that happening in your trial—falling for the stereotype that it would be a woman. Half the jury are women. Coincidentally, Kelly has long blond hair. Lots of women have long blond hair. You don't believe that God would actually interact with you through any kind of vision. It's just your imagination running wild.

Ever since my falling out with God began several years before, I had become adept at this type of reasoning, believing there must be a logical explanation for everything, backed by the scientific method. Whatever my vision was, I didn't want it to be from God and thus proof that he wanted to interact with me. I didn't want God in my life anymore. I didn't get the blessed life His preachers promised to those who stayed pure. I performed all kinds of righteous works for Him, but, despite that, I had grown ashamed of the man I was and embarrassed by my failures. As a youth, I denied myself the full range of earthly pleasures only to end up in a passionless, difficult marriage. God had betrayed me. He didn't keep his end of the bargain.

But I didn't deny God's existence—that would be too alarming for my family and friends. They would all have worried about the security of my immortal soul and that my lack of faith would doom me to Hell, where, as the Bible says, there is "weeping and gnashing of teeth."

My wife Molly not only still believed, but credited God for keeping our marriage alive, or at least keeping us from divorce. She prayed earnestly and emotionally for herself, our kids, and me. I saw no reason to disrupt this, especially if Molly's faith was the one thing that kept us out of divorce court.

For the family's sake, I maintained appearances. I still knew enough from my "ideal Christian boy" background that I could participate convincingly in church, and even lead a Sunday School lesson on occasion. Or teach my kids how to memorize a Bible verse. Or sing the bass part of a Christmas hymn. I couldn't outrun my religious background, still living in and among the believers constantly.

God himself, though, was distant. He had long ago stopped work on His creation, watching it from far away—if at all. He declined to intervene, even on behalf of his most devout adherents like me. He was a divine clock maker who wound up the universe and left it to tick-tock away on its own.

Yet for all my reliance on logic, and for all the repression of emotion, I couldn't deny my vision. Standing at my kitchen counter holding the pale blue jury postcard, I had seen the woman crying in the jury room. Now a woman that looked remarkably like her was coming into the jury room each day with me.

Part of my vision also was that I was the foreperson, led difficult deliberations, and handled tough questions from the press. None of that had happened yet, but the thought it might come true as well filled me with dread. The potential for failure in a very public arena was frightening. We could deadlock and force the misery of a retrial on everyone. I could imagine the mocking comments on the internet, blaming us—blaming me—for the failure.

But the real problem I had with my vision was that I didn't want God to become real again in my life. I didn't want Him to interact with me and guide me like I once thought he did. I didn't want to return to the pain of betrayal and blessing withheld. I wanted God at a safe distance where I wished I had kept him all along.

◆　◆　◆

Opening arguments lasted the entire first day of trial. The prosecution, led by Chief Deputy District Attorney John Hower, spent hours out-lining the case against Robert Ray.Unlike the courthouse, Mr. Hower somewhat resembled his Hollywood counterpart. He vaguely remind-ed me of Jack McCoy, the archetype prosecutor from *Law and Order*: a rugged-looking older man dressed in a sharp, dark blue suit, lines of experience etched in his face. He spoke with a deep, gravelly voice that resonated above the background noise of shuffling papers and the squeaky swivel-chairs. He spoke slowly, and backed-up and restarted frequently, as if measuring each sentence to fit in some word limit.

The prosecution came prepared with PowerPoint slides, photos, and charts. They told us about the night of July 4, 2004, at Lowry Park; how Javad and his friends Elvin and Greg were shot, Greg fatally, after a confrontation with two people. Mr. Hower explained that nearly a year later, Javad was just a few days away from testifying against Robert Ray about the shootings in Lowry Park when he and his fiancé Vivian were killed. He argued that Robert Ray didn't pull the trigger, but ordered his henchman, Sir Mario Owens, to do the deed.

Yes, "Sir" is the actual first name of Ray's accused triggerman. When I first heard this, I thought his parents must be very shrewd. Everybody would be forced to call their son "Sir" whether they respected him or not. As it turned out, though, Sir's friends called him "Rio" which is short for "Mario."

Finally, prosecutor Hower explained that at the time, the police did not suspect Rio was connected to the Lowry Park case in any way. They didn't even know his name. Therefore, Rio had nothing to gain by killing Javad, except to stay in Robert's favor, who kept him employed in a lucrative drug-dealing business.

John Hower spoke with confidence, like a man who seemed assured that we would all arrive at the same place he was. He had good right to be. The previous year he successfully prosecuted Sir Mario Owens, getting Owens convicted of the actual killing and sentenced to Colorado's death row where he was awaiting his fate.

Speaking for the defense team that day was attorney Kevin Clarkson, an experienced criminal defense lawyer in private practice in Denver. While John Hower was formal and used voluminous notes, Mr. Clarkson seemed to me to be more relaxed and extemporaneous. According to his introduction days earlier during final jury selection, he was originally from Wyoming. He wore cowboy boots with his pin-striped, dark blue suit.

Before speaking, Mr. Clarkson flipped through several pages of his notepad, scanning them with his brow furrowed and lips pressed together. He had no slides or props. He just stood with his yellow legal-size notepad in hand, its pages fluttering about as he spoke.

"We won't be saying a lot about all the drug charges that Mr. Ray is also on trial for." He leaned against the desk. "We will certainly fight the charge—the false charge—that Mr. Ray ordered Javad Fields to be killed." Clarkson's voice was now rising in volume, suddenly awake and passionate. "Sir Mario Owens acted completely on his own. He's the one responsible. What this case will come down to is whether the prosecution can prove that Robert Ray ordered this killing."

Clarkson paused, and he scanned the jury box, stopping his gaze on me. "And they have no proof that Robert Ray gave the order."

When the opening arguments for the defense were finished, Judge Rafferty turned toward us and explained we were done for the day and the first witnesses would come the next day. Then he read a little lecture we heard every day at adjournment:

"We are going to adjourn for the day in case 06CR697, People vs. Robert Ray. As you leave for the day, you are to adhere to the following instructions. You are not to form any opinions or make up your mind about the case until all the evidence is heard and you are dismissed for deliberations. You are not to read about the trial or listen to or watch any media stories about it. You are not to conduct your own research, look for evidence, or visit any of the places mentioned in the testimony. You are not to discuss the trial with anyone. You will not email, blog, Facebook, or tweet any information or thoughts about this trial. If anyone contacts you about the trial, you are to report that to me as soon as possible."

The judge peered over the top of his glasses at us and said, "Twit, Tweeter, Facebooker—I don't even know what those are. My bailiff, who is much younger than I and a whiz with all this internet stuff, writes this for me and I just read it." A few cautious laughs came from some of the jury members at this comment, the first laughter I heard all day.

We stood together and walked in an orderly line out of the jury box and disbursed into the hallways of the courthouse. I drove home into the sun as it neared the mountains.

This is going to be easier than I thought, I said to myself as I squinted in the bright sunshine.

Everyone agreed that Robert Ray was not at the crime scene. Someone else pulled the trigger. All we on the jury had to do was determine if Robert had ordered the shooting or not. My nerves subsided as I became enmeshed in the details of the case.

◆ ◆ ◆

"Your honor, the people call Sheri Majors." Mr. Hower, the prosecutor, called the first witness of the trial. I turned to a fresh page in my notebook and wrote "April 9" on the top line. Then in the margin, I wrote a "1" and circled it, for witness number one. I had no way of knowing then that ten weeks later, I would wearily scrawl "111" in the margin as the last witness took the stand.

"Ms. Majors, please state and spell your name for the record," Mr. Hower said.

She leaned forward to the microphone, her eyes directly on John Hower. She cleared her throat. "Sheri Majors." Her voice was shaky. "Sheri. S-h-e-r-i. Majors. M-a-j-o-r-s."

She slumped down in the chair, only her head and shoulders visible above the wood panels that shrouded the witness stand. She looked to be in her mid to late thirties and wore her dark hair pulled away tightly from her face into a ponytail. Her skin slowly drained of color. Mr. Hower tried a few easy questions to get her settled in—where she lived (in a townhome at the corner of Dayton and Idaho Streets), what she did for a living (elementary school teacher).

"Are you nervous about testifying?" Hower walked from the podium to the center of the room.

"Yes." Sheri locked her gaze on Hower, following him as he walked.

"Is it fair to say that you do not want to testify?"

Sheri swallowed hard. "Yes."

I knew since the beginning that Robert Ray was accused of murdering a witness. Now, with this first witness of the trial, I began to understand the magnitude of what Sheri Majors was experiencing. She was nervous, her gaze locked away from Robert Ray because now *she* was the witness, sitting just a few feet in front of an accused witness killer. She looked like someone from my neighborhood, like so many young moms my wife and I knew from church. I felt sorry for her, thinking that she would be looking over her shoulder a lot in the coming months.

Sheri's palpable fear in front of Robert Ray made the charges against him come to life. This was no longer an abstract charge. Suddenly I wondered if I should be afraid as well. Perhaps I should watch my back as I came and left the courthouse. Would I end up like this first witness, nervous and afraid for my safety?

I had to put the thought out of my mind as soon as I could. I turned back to the pages in my notebook, trying to focus on what she was saying. I began to write down everything I was hearing:

Sheri Majors. Lived in townhomes at Dayton/Idaho June 20, 2005. Exhibit 138 townhome area map. Lived in corner unit. 3 more exhibits—photos of Javad's car, shot up in the intersection. Doors open. Blood.

The prosecutors presented photos of Javad's car during Sheri's testimony because she was one of the first people to respond to the gunshots that took the life of Javad and his fiancée Vivian on June 20, 2005. Javad and Vivian were shot as they drove through the intersection of Dayton and Idaho streets, just a few yards from Sheri's townhome.

Javad's gold Chevrolet Monte Carlo was a college graduation gift from his mother, Rhonda Fields. Javad graduated from Colorado State University six weeks earlier and was immensely proud of the car. It was not merely a car. It represented his hard work and achievements in school, graduating in four years with a degree in Speech Communication. The car represented his bright future. He took exceptionally good care of it, keeping cleaning supplies and rags in the trunk so they would always be at hand. Whenever he needed to wait for someone in a parking lot, he would use the time to shine-up his car.

Javad and his fiancée Vivian planned to drive that car to Virginia to visit her brother, a Navy officer. There were job leads for Javad there, and a good school for Vivian to finish her master's degree in nutrition.

The future was wide-open for these newly-minted college graduates. Many community leaders expected Javad to become a public leader and an example for other black young men to follow. The Colorado Black Chamber of Commerce had recently named Javad to its list of "most promising young leaders." Javad and Vivian were ready to start a new life together near the nation's capital. But first Javad had one thing left to do in Colorado, something he had to do out of loyalty to his friend Gregory Vann. He promised to testify in court about what he saw in Lowry Park that July Fourth night almost a year before.

The evening of June 20, 2005, just a few days before the court date for his testimony, Javad and Vivian were in the car on their way to meet some friends for a late dinner. As they approached the intersection of Dayton and Idaho streets, a dark maroon sedan pulled up alongside the Monte Carlo. Through the open passenger window of the dark sedan, a figure appeared wearing a black baseball cap. The figure leaned out the window with an arm extended just a few feet from Javad, gun in hand. We spent a week hearing the testimony of Sheri Majors, Brian Hilliard, and more than a dozen others who were present at the crime scene as they described what happened next.

Sheri Majors recalled hearing the sharp, popping sounds of gunfire at approximately 8:55 p.m., right outside her townhome window.

OneTwoThreeFourFiveSixSevenEight. Then there was a pause for two or three seconds. Then more gunfire, this time louder than the first. OneTwoThreeFourFiveSix.

Sheri's next-door neighbor, Brian Hilliard, also heard the gunshots. He jumped up from his couch and out his front door in seconds. When he testified, he spoke of seeing a dark maroon car as it sped away, a baseball cap flying off the head of someone leaning out the passenger window. Then he noticed the gold Chevrolet. With no regard for his own safety, he darted into the street and sprinted toward the still-moving car as it coasted along slowly. He pulled open the driver's side door. Bracing himself against the door frame, he managed to slow the car to the point where he could lean across the driver and slam the transmission into park. He told us he didn't remember how he was able stop the car, other than perhaps he was possessed of some superhuman strength for a moment. When the car stopped, Brian looked down as he caught his breath, still leaning across the driver.

Stretched out just inches beneath Brian was Javad, twisted away from him with the upper half of his body resting behind the passenger seat. Brian noticed that the driver's seat was reclined almost all the way back, smeared bright red. "Hello! Are you all right?" Brian yelled.

There was no response—only a gurgling sound from Javad's throat. Then Brian heard a moan just inches away from his ear. He jumped back, startled to see a woman in the passenger seat, slumped against the seat belt. It was Vivian. She was wearing shorts, and the top of her legs were bleeding, streaked red with cuts. She moaned again.

Just then the passenger door opened. A woman appeared, kneeling beside the passenger seat. It was Sheri Majors. "Are you okay?" she asked Vivian.

Vivian lifted her head looking panicked and fearful, but she only moaned—no words. Sheri looked inside the back of the car and noticed

Javad lying across the center console, his head resting behind the passenger seat. Javad didn't move and made no sound. Sheri presumed he was dead, so she turned her attention back to Vivian, and tried to make eye contact with her. Vivian's eyes rolled around aimlessly, and her moaning stopped. She took a huge gulp. Her lips moved slightly, silently.

This is bad, Sheri thought to herself as she unbuckled the seat belt. "Help is coming," she said to Vivian. "Hang in there, sweetie."

Sheri looked for a place to perform CPR, and she yelled at Brian for help moving Vivian out of the car. By the time Sheri and Brian removed Vivian from the car, the paramedics arrived and took over. They performed CPR on Vivian all the way to the emergency room.

At the ER, a trauma surgeon tried to save Vivian's life, cutting open her chest to directly shock the heart into beating again. As she died, her eyes rolled back, and her neck strained as she tried to look behind her. Vivian didn't utter a single word, although she desperately tried for the last few minutes of her life.

Javad was sent to the hospital in a separate ambulance. Blood glistened in Javad's mouth. He was drowning in his own blood. They pushed an intubation tube into Javad's throat, placed a ventilator mask over his face, and used a pump to try to get air down the tube and into the lungs. This effort didn't help. A paramedic sliced open Javad's shirt with scissors and saw that the skin on Javad's chest had swelled up, giving the appearance of bubble wrap. Air escaped from Javad's punctured lungs, pushing up on his skin from underneath. The lungs could no longer hold air, even with ventilation.

When Javad arrived at the hospital, the trauma surgeons cut open his chest immediately to try to directly stimulate the heart, the last and most desperate act to save someone's life. Javad died with a tube jammed in his throat, his chest ripped open, and blood-filled lungs.

During the testimony, I looked at Robert Ray for any reaction. He sat quietly, nearly motionless. Rarely, he looked at the witnesses, but when he did there was no hint of expression on his face. He never winced at the sight of a crime scene photo or shook his head in disbelief. No tears welled up in his eyes.

I wanted evidence that this was affecting him in some way—any way. Even a smirk at a witness trembling in fear before him or rolling his eyes at the zealous statements of the prosecutors. Was *anything* getting through to him? Was he so dead inside that not even this horrendous trauma could rouse him even a little?

Molly had often said things just to get a rise out of me, to see if I connected with the pain she was going through in our marriage. This tactic rarely worked, and I wouldn't react.

Was I as calloused as Robert Ray? Could anyone recognize that I was a human capable of reacting humanely to betrayal, hurt, and loss?

If I wanted to see this emotion in an accused murderer, I thought, imagine how much those in my life would want to see it from me.

◆　◆　◆

When it came time to show the jury the autopsy photos, the families of Javad and Vivian were not in the courtroom. We soon understood why.

First, we saw pictures of Vivian, her naked body stretched across a steel table, the top of her legs reddened from the shower of glass that landed on her lap. A taut red streak splayed across the soft brown skin of her left shoulder where a bullet cut a sharp path before diving down into the base of her neck. A crudely stitched gash was above her left breast. Her head rested on a blue block of Styrofoam to keep it off the steel table, her black hair still pulled back into a ponytail the way it was the night she died. Most haunting were her eyes. They were still open and she seemed to be staring up and behind her, like she was still looking helplessly for Javad as she was pulled from the car.

Javad laid on a table next to his fiancé. His fatal wound was on his left side, just below his armpit. The coroner had pulled back layers of skin and pushed aside the muscles to retrieve the bullet. Then he had stitched Javad's side back together coarsely with thick, black thread.

The coroner explained that nothing could have saved Javad. His key arteries were sliced apart by the bullet, his lungs punctured. As the shots flew, he turned to his right, instinctively twisting away from the gunfire, throwing his left arm up to protect his head. This exposed his left side to the killer, and the bullet pierced the car door, the armrest, and his torso. Another bullet struck Javad in the back. The coroner had turned Javad over for a picture of it, and I saw something then that stunned me.

Across his shoulders, Javad had a tattoo directly above the bullet wound. Stretching from his left shoulder to his right was the word *Sacrifice.* The word was written in an ornate script, like Old English letters. The letters were tall and bold, a dark black against his brown skin. Anyone who saw him shirtless when he was alive would have been able to read the word from many yards away.

The coroner didn't mention the tattoo or even pause in his testimony. He kept pointing out more punctures, scrapes, and tears. But I didn't really hear anything else he said. I was transfixed on the word *Sacrifice* etched indelibly in Javad's flesh. I wondered when he had gotten the tattoo. How long before his death? Had he thought sacrifice was his destiny? Javad was laying on that steel table as an actual sacrifice for justice. He had promised he would testify for his fallen friend Greg Vann, and it had cost him his life.

I was jostled out of my trance by the juror sitting next to me, a woman in her seventies and the oldest member of the jury.

"Oh," she said in a voice I'm not sure she realized was audible. "Oh, oh, oh," she repeated, her hand over her mouth, her eyes blinking back tears as she looked at the photo of Javad.

The judge noticed the reactions of us jurors to the autopsy photos, so he dismissed us for a break. We marched glumly into the jury room. Nobody said a word. Normally, our breaks were filled with jurors scrounging through some of the snacks we took turns buying, chatting about the weather or if the food in the cafeteria looked safe to eat. Some might read a magazine or the day's newspaper, stories about the trial cut out of it by the court staff. Everyone stayed quiet now. Some jurors sat slumped in their chairs, staring at the table. Others stared out the window and off into the distance, looking at nothing in particular. I sat staring at the building next to the courthouse.

The Arapahoe County Courthouse sits next to an illustrious neighbor: the headquarters and practice facilities of the Denver Broncos Football Club. Our jury room overlooked the jail on one side and the practice fields on the other. Those of us who followed the National Football League joked about the close proximity of an NFL team to a jail. NFL players ended up in the news frequently for various legal troubles. A popular fan web site displayed a "days since last arrest" counter, marking how long it had been since an NFL player was arrested. I never saw it get past one hundred days.

We were not in a joking mood now. As we sat contemplating the autopsy, a few players gathered on the field, getting ready for their upcoming spring training program. They laughed and threw footballs around, while another player dragged a blue plastic barrel full of footballs onto the field.

From the stony silence of the jury room, I sat and watched these professional athletes frolic in the sunshine on a perfect green field. We were just a hundred yards away, separated by a parking lot. Yet the job I was doing was so vastly different than theirs and in such different worlds. They might as well have been kicking their footballs on the moon. Just how were these multimillionaire athletes earning their money, anyway? By playing a game. And when they were done with a game, what was left? Nothing. It was just entertainment for a few hours.

This didn't seem right to me. How could there could be such carefree millions being thrown at sport while on the other side of the parking lot in our courtroom we were confronting a world of hurt? Here we contemplated two promising lives lost and dozens, if not hundreds, of people traumatized by a heinous crime.

One of the players kicked a football high into the blue sky. I wanted to smash open the window and scream, "It's just a fucking game!"

How could they? How could they, these wealthy ball players, tossing around a stupid leather bag filled with air? Did they not realize what was happening right next to them?

While they were out playing, we were struggling with shattered glass. Bullet casings covering the ground. A car door pock-marked with a dozen bullet holes. Blood soaked into the leather upholstery of a college graduation gift. Bodies torn open. Lungs filled with blood. Eyes rolled back. Two young lovers dead and cold on matching stainless-steel tables. Couldn't the world just pause for a moment? Did no one care about what we had just seen in those photographs and heard from the strained voices of terrified witnesses? Was nobody moved like I was by the word *Sacrifice* tattooed on the back of a man—a witness—killed in a flurry of gunfire?

This simmering rage surprised me. I don't usually react, lose my cool, or get mad—even when people try to provoke me. I actually loved the Broncos and have watched their games faithfully my entire life. I couldn't remember feeling this fury about anything before.

Sure, I knew what anger was. If someone told me "I'm angry," I could deduce in my hyper-logical mind what they were expressing, and what might have made them feel this way, contrasting their expectations with reality. But I had never felt this myself—to feel my face go hot, my teeth grind together, and my muscles clench. And I never felt the desire to yell a curse word at someone, especially the mother of all swear words: *fuck*. For the first time, I felt real and true anger.

The word *sacrifice* is what set me off. I had always felt that my life was a sacrifice, for God and his church. Sacrifice was a common theme in my life. The church preached about it. The church even sang about it. I remembered one of those songs. In 1999, nearly two years after Molly and I were married, a new worship song pervaded the evangelical church. It was called "Lord I Offer My Life." You could go to any evangelical church then and you were almost certain to hear it. The chorus actually described what we were to do—offer our lives *as a pleasing sacrifice.*

This is exactly what I had done with my life—offer it to the Lord. I devoted my time to spreading the Gospel, serving on mission trips, memorizing scripture, and teaching in the church. More than that, I sacrificed my own desires to align with God's word. I stayed away from alcohol, parties, R-rated movies, and anything else that sounded like fun. I not only led a chaste life, I was the very public spokesperson and example for "sexual purity."

For what glory did God use my "pleasing sacrifice?" I was in a difficult marriage, struggling to relate in any way to my wife. With each tear-stained outburst from my disappointed wife, I withdrew ever further into a bitter disillusionment with God. But my sacrifice did not cost me my life. And even with all the difficulties, Molly still had the ring on her finger, the ring I had given her in front of 500 people at a church glowing with Christmas candlelight. I still had my two children, healthy and safe. And a job. As I looked at Javad's torn and battered body, I realized that his death is what a real sacrifice looks like, and I still had a chance to make things better.

As the trial continued over the next few days, we heard from witnesses who knew Javad, including his friends from childhood and college. They called him "Rock" because of his steady character and total dependability. He pushed people to achieve more. He called his old college roommate every day at 7 a.m. to ask, "The day is starting! What are you going to do with it?" He started a business each summer with his friends, so they could earn money for college together. That is why they were at Lowry Park on July 4, 2004, running an entertainment event for dozens of young men and women.

When he died, Javad was on his way to comfort a friend who had just endured a breakup with his long-time girlfriend. Witness after witness said the same thing: Javad was an encouragement to everyone, and a friend to anyone, no matter their background or flaws. The world was diminished with him gone. Javad's life had meaning to many other people. The trial could have easily doubled in length if all who were touched by his life had the chance to testify.

As I drove home after a long day of testimony, I called my wife and offered to pick up food for dinner. I pulled into the parking lot of a grocery store and parked facing west toward the mountains. I turned off the car and sat there for a few minutes, staring ahead. I took a deep breath and let out a heavy sigh. My anger subsided along with the desire to smash a window and tell football players to fuck off. Instead, I felt a heavy loss for Javad and the many people whose lives he had touched.

I wandered from aisle to aisle in the store, looking for whatever I had come for. Other shoppers walked past me, pushing their carts, talking on their mobile phones. While I struggled with sacrifice, the rest of the world continued with dinner plans. If it were me on that stainless-steel table, and not Javad, would I have a steady stream of witnesses testify how I was like a rock? Would they remember me as an encourager, as someone who made others better? Would they say they would miss me? Not miss my *example* of righteousness nor miss my *performance* as the ideal Christian young man—but me. Would they miss *me*?

Somewhere in that grocery store, I decided that no, words like *friendliness* and *encouragement* would not be used to describe me. There would be nobody to say, "Carl made me a better person." There might be some people, those like me, who would laud me for taking a bold stand for righteous behavior and showing the world how to follow the Bible's ideals of moral and sexual purity. They would praise my mental toughness and discipline. They might even recall the considerable success in my career. This did not satisfy me any longer. I had earned a lot of trophies, but no love.

I wandered the store feeling petty and small. I desperately wanted my own sacrifice, my life, to be significant to others. To have meaning. To be redeemed.

nine

THAT'S THE GUY

Serving on a jury means waiting. Waiting for everyone to arrive so we can start. Waiting for everyone to get back from lunch. Waiting through the numerous procedural volleys between the attorneys, which we weren't allowed to hear lest it prejudice our minds against one of them. As the trial became measured in weeks instead of days, we ran out of small talk in the jury room during these numerous breaks and delays. We were a large jury, with twelve deliberating jurors and eight alternates (we wouldn't know which of us were deliberating jurors until closing arguments were done). We got to know each other, for better or worse. Polite deference wore thin as everyone settled into habits they preferred. Two groups emerged: the socialites and the loners.

The loners arrived early in the day to claim their favorite chairs in the jury room, along the window or in the corner. They buried their noses in books or magazines and studied them like airline passengers who don't want to interact with those sitting next to them. One juror, who we would later learn was an alternate, sat in a chair near the door, his head leaning against the wall, eyes closed. After a minute or two, he would doze off, his head bobbing slightly before his chin fell to his chest. He wouldn't respond to any greetings, and he never entered into a conversation. I don't remember even as much as a nod of hello from him. He was a statue of a sleeping man who suddenly came alive when the bailiff announced, "They are ready for you now in the courtroom."

Surprisingly, after the first week, I was hanging out with the socialites. This was highly out of character. I don't jump into a new group of people and start to make conversation, much less friendships. It took me a long time to warm up socially, if it happened at all. For the first week of the trial, I disappeared at lunch to be by myself, just like the other loners. I answered email from work during breaks. I would have been quite happy to stay a loner, but something kept nagging at me, more and more each day.

In the vision I had months before the trial, I was the leader or at least at the center of the action. Reporters pressed their way toward me, their microphones shoved toward my face, the harsh glare of camera lights making me sweat. In the vision, I felt like I was responsible. The idea that I would be the one to lead these complete strangers through deliberations was daunting. They did not know me. Why would they follow me? Why would they listen to me?

I typically confronted challenges on my own, not wanting help. I hated group assignments when I was in school, but I could not choose to work alone now. Deliberations are required for a jury, and decisions require unanimity. That means teamwork. If I was going to be the team leader, I wanted to feel connected with these people. After the first week, I began to sit at the table and join in with the socialites.

I didn't want to be on this trial, much less become the foreperson. When I first received my summons, before I knew anything about the trial, I joked with my wife that I could use a nice diversion from my job and my insufferable boss. I figured a week would be about right. But not this. Not two months of agonizing testimony. Not the pressure of life-or-death decisions. Not what my vision had shown me. Building relationships with other jurors did not come naturally for me, especially under such a short time-frame. But I tried anyway, sensing that in the difficult days to come, I would draw on relationships that were based on more than just polite conversation about the weather.

The socialites sat around the table, the loners in the chairs behind us along the walls. We talked about a lot of things—anything except the prohibited topics of the testimony and evidence. We discussed gardening, baseball, hockey, restaurants, our kids (grandkids for some of the older ones), our jobs, our hobbies, and adventures in the mountains and abroad. Some of the women took to evaluating the wardrobes and styles of those in the courtroom. Some of the comments I heard included:

"Does she know that her jacket is way too tight?"

"I should give her the name of my stylist."

"Should you wear cowboy boots with a pin-striped suit?"

What some of the witnesses wore to court raised the eyebrows of a few on the jury. Women with revealing deep necklines and exposed midriffs. Men with ill-fitting suits that looked to be dug out of a dusty box in an attic the night before.

"Does anyone involved in this case actually own a mirror?" one of the socialites said once.

When it came time for lunch, the loners disappeared quickly and quietly, leaving us socialites standing in the jury room, deciding where we should go. Sometimes we piled into a few cars and drove off to nearby restaurants, or we would march down to the lobby cafeteria *en masse*, groups of lawyers parting in front of us and avoiding eye contact. They were prohibited by the judge from communicating with us outside the courtroom. They weren't allowed to even say "hello" or "good morning."

We had been thrown together through the jury selection process, forced to leave our jobs and daily routines. This was now our job. It wasn't a requirement that we all liked each other, but the job would be easier if we did. Those of us who were deliberating jurors would have to come together, whether we liked each other or not, and arrive at a verdict. Our group could be put to the test with a life-or-death decision.

We were already subjected to many days of testimony concerning the murder at the intersection of Dayton and Idaho Streets on June 20, 2005. We knew *what* had happened. Now we would have to confront the bigger question: who was responsible?

◆ ◆ ◆

Somewhere around the third week of trial, the prosecution called Detective Tom Wilson to the witness stand. We had already heard from plenty of detectives about the crime scene. Now Detective Wilson came to tell us about the year leading up to Javad's and Vivian's death. He was the lead investigator in the murder of Gregory Vann, who died in front of his friend Javad at Lowry Park on July 4, 2004.

Detective Wilson told us about a meeting with Javad a week after Greg's death, at the kitchen table of Javad's mother, Rhonda. He described how Javad was still nursing the gunshot wound to his knee, limping around his mother's house, wincing at each step. He then dropped into a chair across the table from Detective Wilson, leaning his crutches against the wall.

"Are you ready?" Detective Wilson was about to lay a series of photographs in front of Javad, each of them showing a young black man with short hair and similar features. He had readied a stopwatch, wanting to see how long it would take Javad to decide if any of the men in the photos were driving the gold-colored Chevrolet Suburban at Lowry Park. After Javad nodded, Detective Wilson laid six photographs on the table.

Javad didn't hesitate. His finger landed with a thump on the table, right on picture number four. "That's the guy."

"Are you sure?" Wilson was surprised. He hadn't even started his watch.

"That's the guy."

At that time, the police didn't know who shot Gregory Vann to death or wounded Elvin Bell and Javad or if there had been one perpetrator or more. Even though there had been a crowd of people at the park that evening, Javad was the only one willing to talk to police.

Detective Wilson explained this information to the jury, slumped in the chair with a sigh of defeat. He wasn't surprised at all by the lack of witnesses. The police often complained that many young people in Aurora were instilled with the mantra that permeates areas with gang activity: *stop snitchin'*. The gangs wanted everyone to know that if you go to the police, you would suffer serious consequences. Robert Ray and his friends had purchased T-shirts at the Aurora Mall, just three miles from where Javad was killed, with the words *Stop Snitchin'* in bold red letters. The T-shirts were punctuated with pictures of bullet holes and the cross-hairs of a rifle scope. This explained how two men could drive erratically across a crowded park where nearly everyone had a camera, get into a fight, and shoot three people—yet nobody had seen anything.

We learned that two other witnesses reluctantly agreed to testify about that night in Lowry Park. After a brief encounter with Robert Ray in the parking lot of the courthouse, one of those witnesses stopped appearing at court hearings. The other was a young man, a recent Army recruit, days away from leaving for boot camp. His car was confined inside the crime scene at Lowry Park, forcing him to talk with the police to retrieve it. He also disappeared, asking his Army superiors for a quick deployment to Iraq.

Both witnesses eventually testified before us, the soldier flown in from Iraq just for his ten minutes of reluctant and sullen testimony.

The soldier arrived bleary-eyed from the long flight, his green uniform jacket somehow still wrinkle-free. He testified that he had seen Robert Ray at Lowry Park, and could identify what Robert had been wearing and the chrome and black color of his gun. He told us that he was afraid Robert would kill him for testifying, so he had skipped town as soon as he could.

I found this to be a striking example of how seriously many youths feared the gangs and drug dealers. Here a young man sat before us in an army uniform, with several combat ribbons above his left breast pocket. He told us that essentially, he would rather leave the country and face combat in some God-forsaken patch of desert thousands of miles from home than testify and face Robert Ray's anger.

I watched Robert's reaction during the soldier's testimony. Robert sat expressionless as usual, calmly watching and listening. He didn't seem angry or worried or anything, yet the soldier practically sprinted off the witness stand when he was dismissed. He was apparently more eager to face combat in the desert rather than to sit in front of Robert Ray and talk about Lowry Park. I wondered if Javad had the same fear of Robert. If he did, how did he remain so steadfast in his decision to testify?

The *stop snitchin'* crowd in Aurora had apparently not encountered someone of Javad's mettle before. His mother, Rhonda Fields, was determined to raise Javad and his older sister Maisha in what she called a "principle-centered home." She told us on the witness stand how she raised her son and daughter, making many sacrifices so they could live in the "nice part" of Aurora where her kids could attend the excellent Cherry Creek school district. She never said to her kids, "*if* you go to college." She always said, "when." Most importantly, she taught her children to be people of courage and integrity.

Helping her with this mission was Rhonda's father, Booker Marshall. Because Javad's father was out of the picture, Booker, Javad's grandfather, had become his father figure. Booker was a retired Army sergeant, a no-nonsense man with a clear idea of right and wrong. He set an example for Javad of duty, loyalty, and hard work. He told Javad that nobody was going to give him anything, teaching him that he would need to earn his way in the world. Javad did just that, working as a caddy at Denver Country Club and starting business ventures with his friends. When Javad and Maisha graduated from Colorado State University, the entire family was immensely proud. It seemed that every other picture we saw of Javad or Maisha featured them wearing a cap and gown.

I recognized similarities between the Fields family and my own. My father and grandfathers had also served in combat. We believed in the same values of duty, honor, and hard work. I had worked my way to a college degree at the same school as Javad, also raising my own funds. But I had not been tested like Javad. As I listened to the testimony about Javad's life, I thought how easy it was to preach these values but wondered if I would be willing to uphold them to the point of death.

These values compelled Javad to speak to Detective Wilson when nobody else would have come forward. While his courage was remarkable, Javad had very little to say to the detective. He had not seen who shot him or his friends. The only thing he had described with certainty was the driver of the getaway vehicle.

That's the guy—Robert Ray.

With this as their only piece of eyewitness evidence, the Arapahoe County District Attorney decided to try Robert Ray for accessory to murder. Javad, and the moment he glimpsed Robert Ray behind the wheel of the Suburban, was essentially their entire case. They didn't have the gold-colored Suburban, the murder weapon, or any other witnesses.

Robert hired a famous Denver attorney, a celebrity lawyer who normally represented Denver's professional athletes in their scrapes with the law. It wouldn't have been hard for any lawyer to discredit

Javad's testimony, especially not a superstar like this. Javad had just been shot, and it was dark, so how could he have been sure it was Robert driving the vehicle? This was by no means an open-and-shut case, and even if Robert was convicted, he would have faced a maximum of only six years in prison.

Surprisingly, those odds had not been good enough for Robert Ray. Like the lawyer's other clients, Robert was wealthy. He had made a fortune by selling cocaine. Much of his family was involved in his drug business, too. The clan had moved to Aurora from the south side of Chicago and was prospering in a relatively competition-free atmosphere for drug dealers. Robert used two businesses as fronts, a barbershop and a recording studio, to distribute cocaine to a small network of dealers. Robert made $40,000 a month in cash, tax free of course.

As I listened to the story of Robert's success, I realized that he and Javad shared the same value of hard work. They just applied it to radically different channels.

Robert was understandably reluctant to give up his cash cow. As unlikely as a conviction would have been, even a short stint in prison would cost Robert his empire. That's why that one moment at his mother's kitchen table was the beginning of the end for Javad. At that point, Robert began a year-long campaign of bribery and intimidation to squelch Javad's testimony. To avoid being implicated in any witness tampering, Robert ensured he was never seen anywhere near Javad. Through surrogates, Robert offered Javad $10,000 to skip out on his testimony.

When that hadn't worked, Robert's family, including his wife, sisters-in-law, and half-brother, started trailing Javad, seeking him out in public places, glaring at him menacingly. When that failed to scare Javad away, Robert offered ten thousand dollars to anyone who would "take Javad out." Nobody took him up on the offer. As the trial drew closer, Robert ran out of ideas.

On Father's Day 2005 (Sunday, June 19), Robert and three of his crew were sitting in the parking lot of Gibby's, an Aurora sports bar. Javad, along with his fiancé Vivian and some friends, were inside playing pool and drinking beer. With the trial set to begin later that week, Robert knew this could be his last chance to change Javad's mind about testifying. But he did not want to risk going in after Javad himself. There would have been too many witnesses inside Gibby's, plus Javad would have recognized him. Robert sent in Perish Carter, his stepbrother.

Perish's own family described him as mentally slow. In the past, Robert had given him only easy tasks to do, like washing cars. He never trusted Perish to handle money, weapons, or drugs, but Perish was the only person left in the posse that Javad had never seen before. This is why Robert sent him into Gibby's to confront Javad, despite his misgivings about Perish's capabilities. As Robert had feared, Perish did not accomplish his task smoothly.

There were several surveillance cameras in Gibby's, and we watched the video in the courtroom. The prosecutors paused the video to point out the identities of the various people we could see in the black-and-white picture. Because the surveillance lacked audio, the prosecution called several witnesses to narrate what we were seeing. These witnesses included the friends of Javad and Vivian who had been playing pool with them, and the owner and manager of the restaurant. This laborious and painstaking narration process meant that we watched this video clip about a dozen times.

We watched as Perish walked into Gibby's, looking around in confusion for a minute or two. He circled the tables and walked past Javad who was at a pool table, beer in hand. Perish finally got tired of searching, so he stopped in the middle of the restaurant and yelled, "Javad! Javad Fields!"

Javad wheeled around and faced Perish. Right there in the middle of that busy restaurant, Perish said to him, "Are you Javad Fields, that nigga who is wanted in the streets?"

Javad set down his drink. Perish walked him over to the front window and pointed to the parking lot. The two of them looked out the window and had a brief conversation. Perish left through the front door and Javad walked quickly over to his group. "We gotta go— now!" he told them.

◆　◆　◆

After the Gibby's testimony was concluded, Maisha Pollard took the stand next. She last spoke to her brother Javad the afternoon of June 20, 2005, the day after the incident at Gibby's. She was sitting in the lobby of her dentist's office when her mobile phone rang. Javad called, and his voice sounded anxious and fearful, an unusual state of mind for him.

"The dudes are after me," he told her.

"What dudes?" Maisha replied. "What are you talking about?"

At that moment, the dentist came into the lobby and called Maisha. Maisha said she would call Javad back. Before they ended the call, Javad said that when they spoke again, he wanted to talk about coming out to California, where Maisha, her husband, and young daughters were living.

Javad called Maisha again, just as she was leaving the dentist. He sounded calmer and he described for his sister what happened the previous day. A group of people were following him around. Someone he didn't know had yelled out his name at Gibby's and had told him he was a marked man.

Maisha was shocked. Right there in her dentist's office she learned for the first time what Javad had endured—the months of bribery, intimidation, and threats. She told Javad to drop everything and go to the airport right away. Their mother Rhonda worked for United Airlines and Javad could use her employee family pass to get on the next flight from Denver to Los Angeles. He could be there within a few hours.

But Javad said no. He was steadfast in his decision to testify, and in his loyalty to Greg Vann, his fallen friend. He thought of California as an escape *after* his testimony. He would hide out until the trial was over, and Robert Ray was hopefully locked away in prison. Then he could safely carry out his plans with Vivian to get married and move east.

Maisha was torn. She wanted her brother to be safe but also understood Javad's character. They had been raised that way, to do the right thing, to live out their grandfather's ideals of duty and honor. They didn't run from a challenge. It helped to hear that Javad's voice was now calm and assured, like normal. If he didn't see a reason to panic, then she wouldn't panic either. She said goodbye to Javad, telling him she would call the next day. She didn't realize Javad had only six more hours to live.

How cruel, I thought, that Maisha had to say goodbye while wrapped up in the middle of routine and mundane activity. How cruel that there was no time for a longer, more meaningful conversation. She didn't know that she was speaking to her brother for the last time, standing in the dentist's waiting room, her mouth still numb from dental work.

◆ ◆ ◆

As I studied the photos and videos from the incident at Gibby's, I noticed that each picture had a time stamp in the lower right corner. I saw a picture of Javad, pool cue in hand, laughing and talking to Vivian and friends. Right below him in the photo, the date and time was printed neatly. In one picture after another the time stamp appeared. It was a clock counting down the final hours of his life.

In his final days, Javad felt he was doomed. He told his friends he was going to die. We heard about this from the testimony of his college roommate.

"This isn't some Hollywood movie," his college roommate once told him. "Nobody is out to get you."

He noticed Javad was driving his car with the seat reclined nearly all the way. He marveled that Javad could see out the window at all. Javad drove like this to minimize his profile in the window and thus make himself a smaller target. He thought he was being followed, and in fact, he was. For weeks he carried in his wallet the business card of the Arapahoe County witness protection agent. It was on him the day he died. But he never called. He never once told anyone of the specific threats, except for the panicky phone call he placed to his sister Maisha on the day he died, and another an hour later to his uncle. Javad seemed resigned to a confrontation with Robert Ray—a likely fatal one.

I wondered if Javad was comfortable with the idea of his own death. I would stare at pictures of him from his last days alive and wonder, Javad, are you frightened? Are you satisfied that you have done what you are supposed to do with your life? Are you at peace?

I asked these questions because I was not at peace with the thought of my own death. Maybe I had never been at peace with death. I remembered a frightening moment I had about six years before the trial began. I finished a business trip in Salt Lake City and boarded an airplane for the quick flight back home to Denver. The clouds that day piled high above the Uinta mountains, a billowing, brilliant white against the deep blue afternoon sky. These type of cloud formations indicated turbulent air and thunderstorms, and indeed the pilot had told us all to "expect a few bumps on the climb out."

Sure enough, the airplane rocked lightly as we headed east over the mountains and into the clouds. Then suddenly, there was a loud thump as the airplane bounced up and then dropped back down. The seat belt pressed into my hips as the plane dropped. Another thump and we bounced back up and then down again, even more sharply. An overhead bin ahead of me popped open, and a suit coat and purse spilled out. Many of the passengers gasped. I gripped the armrest tightly and glanced out the window. The tops of clouds leapt up and dashed back down as the plane rocked. One moment blue sky flashed in the window, the next a haze of gray and white, then back again to blue. Another jolt. This time, someone screamed as we slammed into our seat belts again. The aircraft shook, and I pushed my feet into the floor trying to steady myself. The woman seated next to me clenched my forearm as she too tried to grab the armrest between us. Her fingernails dug into my skin.

I had flown all around the world over the years, and for the first time I thought my plane might crash. A wave of thoughts flooded my mind, and panic tightened my chest. I hadn't called my wife that day, and I had left a huge list of unfinished work and repairs around the house. Did I have enough life insurance for two young kids and a stay-at-home mom? Who would tell my family? How would they react? Would they find my body in the wreckage? Most frightening of all, I thought *I haven't done enough*. In that moment, I saw my life unfinished and full of failures I wanted to repair.

Suddenly, I started praying. Not aloud, just whispering to myself, my lips barely moving. *Lord Jesus, please protect us.* Another jolt. *Lord Jesus, please protect us.* The airplane shook again as we bounced up and down. *Lord Jesus, please protect us.* I kept repeating this little prayer over and over. It was all I could do.

The entire turbulent episode lasted maybe a minute. The thuds and jolts and wild swings subsided as we punched out over the clouds.

A voice came over the sound system. "Ladies and gentlemen, from the cockpit, this is the captain speaking." His voice was a Texas drawl. "Well that sure was exciting! And now you know why we tell you folks to keep those seatbelts fastened."

There was a smattering of nervous laughter among the passengers. My seatmate relaxed her grip on my forearm and looked at me. There were deep red semicircles where her fingernails had dug in.

"Sorry about that," she said with a sheepish grin.

The Texas drawl came back over the speakers. "We should be back in smooth air here in a moment. You might be wondering about this aircraft and let me assure you, it is built to take this kind of turbulence. This isn't even the worst turbulence I've seen this year."

As we landed in Denver, I walked through the concourse, my legs rubbery from the stress. I thought about the praying I had done during the turbulence. By that point in my life, I was done with God and prayers, believing that God doesn't intervene, and miracles were a thing of the storybook past. So why did I pray? I didn't understand it.

This type of panic-induced prayer would continue every time I stepped on an airplane after that. I began to repeat the same little prayer silently to myself as I walked down a jetway and onto a waiting aircraft:

Lord Jesus, I want so much to return home safely to my family. Please give me a safe journey today. Please protect this aircraft—keep it in safe and perfect working condition. Please protect the crew—keep them awake and alert to danger. Please protect us in the weather—give us a safe and smooth flight. And Lord Jesus, if there is anyone who wants to do us harm on this flight, I pray you completely stop their plans and give us a safe arrival.

While I never experienced turbulence again like I did on that flight from Salt Lake City, if I did feel the plane start to shake, I began my chant again: *Lord Jesus, please protect us.*

This was bizarre and completely illogical behavior for me. I had long before stopped believing in prayer and a God who intervened in my life. I was also a private pilot, having obtained my license when I was an Air Force ROTC cadet in college. I knew how turbulence worked. I had experienced it many times in "bug smasher" aircraft a fraction the size of an airliner, with no panic or problems. I once attempted a landing in a small four-seat Cessna during crosswinds so strong, I couldn't stay lined up with the runway and had to divert to an airport twenty miles away. I felt like I was riding a kite, not piloting an airplane. Despite my experience as a pilot, after that Denver flight

I boarded modern jet aircraft acting like a devout Catholic praying the rosary. I was relieved whenever a business trip was cancelled since that was one less flight I had to take.

I thought about this as I studied the final time-stamped photographs of Javad. In the jury box, we were bombarded with images of death. What was it about death that really spooked me? I realized what really frightened me was loss of control. This is why I didn't mind the turbulence when I was in the pilot's seat—I was at the controls of the airplane. This is why the drive to the airport didn't scare me, even though statistically it was far more dangerous than even the most turbulent flight. I was in the driver's seat. Flying as a passenger scared me because I realized I was not in control.

When I acted as the "ideal Christian boy," I could largely control my life. My achievements and greatness were up to me. But when I married, there was now another person directly involved in my life every day. I could not control her. I hurt and disappointed her and I couldn't simply work my way back to success. She desired things from me that were beyond my capabilities. Relying on willpower alone to mend my shortcomings was not enough. I no longer had control over every aspect of my life. My ability to carefully avoid failure and shame was lost. No longer could I cultivate an image of perfection.

Why didn't Javad take control?

This is what bothered me about the time-stamped pictures of Javad. He could have fled to California, like his sister urged him to. He could have skipped out on his testimony and hardly anyone would have blamed him. Javad told his friends and family time and again, he *must* testify against the killers who took the life of his friend Greg. This was not negotiable. At that time, testifying was his purpose and he would not be deterred, even if it meant giving up control. Javad did not want to die, and he had longer-term plans. But Javad was a man of purpose and values, and he was remembered and celebrated for it. Courage isn't required when you have control. I no longer had control.

But I didn't have courage, either. And I was not satisfied that I had accomplished my life's purpose.

The trial entered a gloomy, frightening phase. Every hour in the courtroom brought with it another reminder of tragedy and death. The door from Javad's car, pock-marked with bullet holes, was brought in and leaned against the courtroom wall. Stashed in a corner were life-size mannequins representing Greg, Javad, and Vivian with dowels stuck in them to demonstrate the angle of each bullet as it punctured their bodies. Sealed bags of blood-stained clothing and bullet casings sat on a cart that we walked past on our way in and out of the courtroom. Then joining the piles of evidence were the photos of their last day alive, timestamps and all, from a strip-mall sports bar.

As I left the courthouse during those days of testimony, I began to study the traffic around me, checking the rearview mirror frequently, looking for suspicious vehicles. I took different routes home, afraid someone might be studying my routines to ambush me. As I approached my house, I would slow down, looking for any cars I didn't recognize before slipping into the garage and closing the door quickly. I had no reason to believe I was being followed or threatened, but I was spooked anyway.

A good Christian shouldn't be filled with fear of death. Christians go to Heaven when they die. What could be better than that? In evangelical circles, it is very common to hear someone say they are willing to live for as long as the Lord wants, but they would rather die and go to be with him in Heaven. They love to quote the Apostle Paul: "For to me, to live is Christ, and to die is gain" (Philippians 1:21).

Very few people in my world knew the Bible better than me, yet this verse made no sense. This longing for death mystified me. How could anyone be at peace with their own death? Even if death meant ascending to Heaven, I didn't want to die.

Beyond the lack of control, another aspect of death I feared was judgment. The scriptures say: "It is appointed for men to die once, and after this comes judgment" (Hebrews 9:27). The Bible is clear that everyone will be judged by God at the end. At stake is the eternal resting place for the soul: Heaven or Hell. This is the "judgment day" that even non-Christians have heard of. As ominous as it sounds, I didn't fear this divine judgment. Instead, I was more afraid of the judgment of mere mortals.

◆ ◆ ◆

The fundamentalist Christian teachings common in my youth held that personal failings, such as a divorce, were usually the result of sin blocking the blessings of God. Strict obedience to God's laws, and the authority of male leadership in the church and the home, provided an "umbrella of protection" to the faithful. Step out from under the umbrella at your own risk. I learned this teaching at a young age, and it fueled my legalism—focusing on adherence to the laws spelled out in the Bible. It fueled my judgmental outlook on others. I didn't think I was being judgmental, and neither did anyone else I knew at church. Instead, we viewed preaching and moralizing as an act of love. Someone had to warn others that the lives they were living were dangerous. If we truly loved humanity, our reasoning went, shouldn't we want to tell others that they were missing out on God's blessings? That they could be risking eternity in Hell?

There was no end to the list of sins that we needed to preach about. Some of them were big, political topics, like gay rights, which of course, we were against. Others were more practical, like the type of clothing women and girls should wear. While modest dress might seem like a modest topic, it was actually of extravagant importance to us. If women dressed immodestly, it could cause a man to stumble into lust. Lust leads to sexual sins like promiscuity and adultery. Promiscuity and adultery lead to the breakdown of the family unit, which we viewed as the bedrock of the country and civilization itself.

As a result, there were no small subjects. Every rule was an important stitch in the fabric that held society together.

Criticizing what a girl wore, or even sending her home to change her outfit from a "revealing" one to a "modest" one, was as important as caring for the poor.

Avoiding R-rated movies was important to keep the mind focused on holy and righteous thoughts, not thoughts of sex, drugs, or profane language.

Prohibiting earrings on men was important because we had heard somewhere that a man with an earring was signaling that he is gay.

Rejecting gambling was important because it wasted resources (money) that God had entrusted to us.

Abstaining from alcoholic drinks was important because that is the only way to guarantee staying clear of the sin of drunkenness.

The list had no end. This is the essence of legalism in the evangelical, fundamentalist church.

Staying away from sin was not good enough, though. I wanted to "avoid even the appearance of evil." Reputation was of utmost importance because, after all, we were preaching a high standard of moral purity. As a young man, I put all my effort into being "the ideal Christian boy," and my reputation was golden. As an adult in my late thirties, my personal failings embarrassed and hurt me.

What would people in the church think if they saw my wife crying on our green leather couch, mourning her emotional devastation?

What would they say if they knew at one point she wanted our marriage to be over (even if it meant death!) because it was so dysfunctional?

How would their opinion of me change if they knew that God had not blessed our marriage?

The dissonance between my Christian reputation and reality drove my fear of death. This was the scariest thing of all—to be revealed for all I had done or, more importantly, all I had not done. To be discussed and judged with no chance ever again to make amends. To be ashamed and exposed.

I had tried to be the ideal Christian but was not satisfied with what I had become. I was not ready for someone to rummage through my life and discover I was a fraud. For all my preaching as a youth about God's gift of sex and its proper place—marriage—I was a married man paralyzed with sexual dysfunction. For all my good deeds at the pulpit and on the mission field, I was not happy, even though we all affirmed "the joy of the Lord is our strength." I had no real joy in my righteous life. I was jealous of those, Christian or not, who enjoyed life and had fun. Many of them had better marriages than I had, even after a youth of promiscuity and living in sin.

For all the large swaths of the Bible I had memorized, I was a doubting Thomas with a faith in God that was diminishing every day. If I died that day in a plane crash, I would depart unsatisfied and feeling like a failure. I was not ready to die because I did not want to be judged.

As we neared closing arguments nearly a month into the trial, the irony of my fears was not lost on me. Having grown up in the evangelical church, I had the credentials to be an excellent judge of a sinner, but I wanted nothing to do with judgment any more. Until this trial, I never had to see the actual results of judging a person, even with all the preaching I had done about sin and proper choices in life. No sinners hung out with me. Why would they? Disconnected from those I judged, I never had to witness the havoc my words and attitudes might have had on another person. I never saw the hurt, and I never needed to empathize.

Because of the trial, I would see the consequences of my judgment first hand. A man might be declared guilty and spend the rest of his life in prison or even be put to death. I sat in a position of enormous power, but I didn't feel powerful. Being a judge could not protect me from my fear of judgment.

◆　◆　◆

"Hey Ellie, could you come downstairs for a minute?" I yelled up the stairs for my eight-year-old daughter.

It was a Saturday morning. She came bounding down the stairs, blond hair bobbing up and down, just above her shoulders.

"What?" She took the final step with a jump, landing on both feet on the wood floor in the hallway.

"I need to talk to you about your birthday party."

Her eyes widened. "I'm turning nine years old in exactly eight days."

"Yes, I know, but Mom and I were thinking that we could do a much better party a bit later in the year—maybe in a month or two. If we try to put it together now with only eight days to go, well, we're just not going to be able to do a good job with it."

Ellie looked down a bit. She clasped her hands in front of her and pushed them down until her arms were straight. She twisted back and forth slightly.

"It's just been so busy with Mom going back to work, your cousins here, me working on a jury."

It had been a crazy month. After taking a few years off to stay at home with our kids, Molly was getting ready to return to work as a high school math teacher. She had been interviewing for jobs while I was starting on the jury and had just received an offer from the highly-rated high school a mile down the street—her dream job. We hadn't celebrated yet. My sister, recovering from divorce, had moved in to our home with her three young kids and a dog while she found a new place to live. On top of all that, the trial.

Ellie glanced up at me. "What's a jury?"

I thought for a moment. "Well, I'm not doing my normal job…"

"Your computer job?"

"Right. Instead, I'm on a jury for a while. In a courtroom. With lawyers and police officers."

Ellie seemed concerned. She cocked her head. "Are you in trouble?"

"No, I'm not in trouble. The judge and the lawyers asked me to help them decide if someone is guilty or not guilty of a crime." Ellie's concerned look hadn't gone away. "Being on a jury is something lots of people have to do. It's part of being a citizen in the U.S."

"What crime?" she asked.

"It's a secret—ha!" I tried to be funny for a moment, to lighten up the mood. "The judge won't let me talk about it until the whole thing is done."

"Why did the judge ask you to be on the jury?" She stopped twisting and looked at me. It was a good question. The interview with defense lawyer flashed into my mind. *Why was I on this jury?*

"Well, maybe they thought I would do a good job. And my regular job will keep paying me, which is good. That makes it easier than for most."

"Oh. Can I go back upstairs now?"

"Yeah, and don't worry, we'll still have a great birthday party for you. It's just gonna' be late. Thanks for understanding."

Ellie bounced back up the stairs on all fours. "Don't go to jail!" she yelled playfully as she disappeared into the upstairs hallway.

The party wouldn't happen until August, four months later. Even if we had somehow found the time to make it work, I was not in the right mental state for a kid's birthday party—not after dealing for weeks with death, grief, and blame. I didn't have enough compartments in my mind to handle autopsy photos, mannequins of the dead, a shot-up car door, and a princess birthday cake all at once.

How much longer could I hold it all in? Everyone else in the case could talk with their friends and family about what they were doing, but not the jury.

Those of us on the jury were about to set aside our normal careers to give a verdict in a murder case. I did my best to hide my trepidation about making such a monumental judgment. I wondered if any of my juror colleagues were feeling like I was. Spooked about judgment and death. Weighed down by life choices. I had no way to tell, since we couldn't talk about it. Technically, we were supposed to switch off all thoughts of what we had seen and heard at the end of each day and carry on as if the trial didn't even exist. We weren't allowed any outlet. We couldn't even tell anyone what trial we were on. I felt incredibly lonely in this juror bubble. Could the other jurors see my struggle?

I saw signs that the stress was getting to the others, too. Stepping away from life for so long had consequences. Dozens of missed appointments. Impacts to careers and incomes. One juror (later to be revealed as an alternate) constantly fretted as important business deals were being made at his office without him. As soon as we were on a break, he would frantically pace the jury room on his mobile phone. Another alternate juror who normally worked day shifts took on night shifts in order to keep his income going, arriving bleary-eyed and exhausted each day. Another juror's income dried up, putting stress on the rest of her family.

The idea of having to judge a man with life-and-death consequences took an emotional and physical toll, too. Two of the jurors who had quit smoking were now stressed enough to take up the habit again, making their way on breaks to the walled-in smoking area of the courthouse. We could pass the time and hide from the reality of our new job for a while, talking about sports or the birds that landed on the fence outside our jury room window.

But we all knew what was coming, even if we weren't allowed to speak of it. Soon the fears and anxieties we all had would come spilling out. And my vision, the one I had months before the trial even began, was about to become very real.

ten

DECISIONS

After nearly a month of testimony, closing arguments in the trial took two days. The prosecutors rehashed every major point they had made in the previous three weeks. They brought up the photographs again, replayed parts of video clips, and referred to the other exhibits that lined the walls of courtroom 201, like the shot-up door from Javad's car.

I tried to take more notes during this barrage of information because I worried I wouldn't remember all the key points. It was hopeless to try and keep up with only pen and paper. After an hour or so, I stopped taking notes, and put down my notebook in favor of just listening. I listened for anything that didn't make sense to me or struck a chord of doubt that Robert Ray was a murderer. The prosecution, apparently sensing what I was thinking, reminded all of us that they didn't have to prove their case beyond all doubt, just beyond *reasonable* doubt. The standard was amazingly vague for such an important decision: to find Robert Ray guilty, there must be enough evidence of guilt, free of any doubt that a "reasonable person" might have.

Naturally, the defense team closed their case by pointing out all the areas where they thought we should have reasonable doubts. Their chief concern was that Robert Ray was not at the crime scene. He had a clear alibi on video. He was at a liquor store at the time of the shooting, recorded on the store's surveillance cameras. Even the prosecution agreed Robert Ray did not pull the trigger. He was guilty of first-degree murder, the prosecution argued, because he ordered and arranged it. The defense countered that there was no evidence of a direct order to kill, or at least the evidence was unreliable, coming from people who would themselves escape prosecution if they testified against Robert Ray. The defense claimed that the killings were all the work of Sir Mario Owens and Owens acted on his own. Robert Ray might have wanted to scare Javad, but not kill him.

The prosecution anticipated that the largely circumstantial case could be a problem for us on the jury. During final jury selection four weeks prior, they asked us many questions about circumstantial evidence. One of the prosecutors leading the jury selection efforts introduced the subject by asking us to imagine we were watching a championship basketball game on television. The score was tied with just seconds to go.

"But then there is a technical glitch with the TV cameras," she said, "and all you can see is a section of the crowd and the sidelines, but not the actual play on the court. Suddenly, the crowd erupts in cheers and the players on one bench leap into the air with joy, hugging each other. The players on the other bench slink off the court, their heads down. Even though you didn't see the play, can you tell what happened anyway?"

Her example proved to be an apt analogy. But the case wasn't as simple as a basketball game. While there was some direct evidence, convicting Robert Ray could only be done by stitching together many pieces of circumstantial evidence, if it could be done at all.

After closing arguments, the judge spent another half-day review-ing the "instructions of law." The instructions were documents typed up and read aloud to us as we followed along with our own copies. They specified the legal criteria that must be met to secure a convic-tion on any of the charges, a dizzying array of rules. They contained, for example, the technical definitions of first-degree murder. The most important instruction was that we had to be unanimous in our findings. To find Robert Ray guilty, all twelve of us had to say so. If not guilty, again all twelve. A split vote would be a mistrial.

The judge also told us to put any thought of punishment out of our minds. Whether we found Robert Ray guilty or not, we must de-cide solely on the evidence. We were not allowed to talk about or even consider in our own minds what would happen to Robert Ray if we decided he was not guilty. Would he be set free? Would he be in prison anyway on other charges? It did not matter. More importantly, we were not allowed to discuss or even think about the punishment Robert Ray would receive if we arrived at a guilty verdict.

I thought this was an impossible demand. We all knew from the beginning that if we found Robert Ray guilty of first-degree murder, there would be another month-long trial. Only this one would focus entirely on the punishment: life in prison without parole or death. We the jury would have to decide between those two options.

I wondered if the other jurors thought what was obvious to me. Find him not guilty, we all go home. Find him guilty, we go back to work for another month, this time with a task harder than the first.

When the judge finished reading to us, he set down his papers and looked our way. "Now it is your turn," he said. "The first step is to determine who should be the foreperson."

First step? I was listening closely for step two, but it never came.

"After selecting a foreperson, you are in charge of the deliberation process," the judge said.

He dismissed us to the jury room. I was amazed. It took four weeks to present the evidence. A half-day to tell us the legal definitions of the crimes charged against Robert Ray. But not one minute on how we were to deliberate. In the business world there are entire seminars, often days in length, on how to conduct meetings and negotiations. But here, no advice. No best practices. Just twelve ordinary citizens, amateurs in the law, told to pick a leader and let the court know when we reached a decision.

I felt angry and afraid all at once. Angry that the pressure was all on us, and yet we were given no help. Afraid that we would crack under the pressure, be unable to reach a decision, and drag the justice system of Colorado into chaos.

The judge also told us that from now on, the jury must stay together. If someone needed a break, we would all have to take a break. There could be absolutely no discussions unless all twelve of us were present.

I marched into the jury room with my eleven new, inseparable co-workers. We took the same seats we had been sitting in since the first week when we all staked out our little conference table territories. The bailiff gave us a two-way radio to call him if we needed something, or to let the court know when we had a verdict. Then he confiscated all our mobile phones. We dropped them into a basket he held out, the plastic clattering as the phones piled up. We were cut off from the outside world.

I sat at the middle of the table facing the window. I could see the county jail and the Denver Broncos' practice facility across the parking lot, the same view I had weeks before when I felt so angry at the football players on the practice fields below me. My seat didn't have the leg and elbow room like the ones at the head and foot of the table, and it was in the center of the room. During every break, a line of jurors squeezed behind my chair to get to the coffee maker. It wasn't the best seat, but I had arrived later than most everyone else on the first day of the trial, and it was the best that was left. Starting to my left, and going clockwise around the table were my eleven new coworkers:

- Tonya, human resources manager at a bank.
- Vicki, receptionist at a local high school.
- Gregory (Greg), computer help desk worker for a state agency.
- Lois, retired school principal.
- James, real estate agent.
- Rebecca, payroll clerk for a family-owned trucking business.
- Marie, assistant manager for a hotel.
- Rick, computer systems analyst for a consulting company.
- Kelly, the youngest in our group and a high school soccer coach.
- Steven, accountant for an insurance company.
- Daniel (Dan), the oldest in our group and an auto body shop manager just a year away from retirement.

As we sat in our large, black leather chairs, the only sounds were of notebooks being set on the table. I shifted in my chair and it creaked. I instantly froze, not wanting the noise to cause people to look my way. Late afternoon sunshine streamed in through the room's south-facing windows and suddenly I felt very warm. The quiet continued for another ten seconds as nobody looked up and nobody moved.

"Well, here we are," said one of the women at last. "Hard to believe this is actually happening."

"Yeah, four weeks," said another voice.

The room went quiet again. No squeaky chairs, no clicking pens, not even any throat clearing. The room seemed to be growing hotter.

Then, in a move that probably sealed my fate, I spoke up. "I guess we are supposed to pick a foreman, or fore*person*, as the judge said." Everyone's eyes were suddenly on me. "Does anyone have a suggestion for how we should pick?"

The other jurors looked around the room at each other, but nobody said anything. "Well, maybe I should ask this first: Does anyone want to volunteer to be the foreperson?"

A few people laughed nervously and extended their hands out as if to say, "Keep that away from me." Nobody spoke up.

I looked to my left directly at Greg, the help desk worker. I don't know why I looked at him, other than he was seated at the head of the table. He shook his head vigorously with a look on his face that said, "Don't look at me!"

Another awkward pause. Apparently, I was going to be the one to push this along.

"Well since nobody wants to volunteer, I suggest we take a vote." There were nods of agreement all around the room. "Everyone write down the name of who you think should be the foreperson and then fold that paper in half and give it to Rebecca to count."

"Why me?" Rebecca had a look of concern on her face.

"Well, because you are often counting and recording time cards."

Rebecca laughed, because it was true. She was trying to keep up with the payroll at her family's trucking business and would often bring in stacks of time cards and other materials to check during lunch and breaks.

We tore pages out of our notebooks for the vote. A minute later Rebecca had twelve slips of paper. She counted them out one by one and then made the announcement.

"Ten votes for Carl, one for Rick, and one for me."

I was not surprised. I had been thinking for weeks about my vision, in which I had stood at my kitchen counter months earlier with the jury summons letter and had seen that this would happen, even before I knew what the trial was about. I thought about everything that had to fall into place for that vision to come true. First, I had to be selected from a pool of 2,000 potential jurors in a three-step process that took the lawyers nearly three months. Then, I had to be placed as a deliberating juror instead of an alternate. Then, everyone else would have to decline the role of foreperson. Finally, the other jurors would have to vote for me, and that just happened.

Steven, the accountant, spoke up when he heard the results of the vote. "Are you guys sure that we don't want anyone, say, a little older to be the foreperson?"

I had voted for Rick, the systems analyst. Now I knew the identity of the other person who did not vote for me. Oh great, I thought to myself, one minute into this and already a conflict. Why did Steven object to me? At thirty-eight, I was one of the youngest jurors in the room. Not old, I thought, but still old enough to hold any public office. Fortunately, I didn't have to think of a response to Steven.

Dan, the oldest of our group and seated to my right, gave me a firm pat on the shoulder with his big left hand. "Well, congratulations! You're the leader now!" That seemed to settle it, as ten others nodded in agreement—everyone but Steven.

"Well thanks, I guess." I tried to sound humorous to take the edge off the situation.

"I'm sure it is a great honor for you!" Dan laughed and squeezed my shoulder. Dan was a big guy with his white hair in a sharp, military style crew cut—an imposing figure. But he had a merry look to his face. With the right beard, he could pass for Santa Claus. Steven didn't appear to want to challenge Santa Claus.

I looked around at the group and saw some jurors propping their heads up with their hands, elbows on the table. Others leaned heavily on the armrest of their chairs, staring somewhere into the middle of the table. Eleven exhausted people. We were hungry, too, sacrificing the lunch hour so Judge Rafferty could finish reading to us the entire Colorado Revised Statutes, or so it seemed.

"We need to start our work on a fresh brain," I announced to the jury. "Let's reconvene tomorrow."

There were sighs of relief around the room. Greg slid the two-way radio across the table to me and I called the bailiff. For my first official act as foreperson, I adjourned us for the day. I could imagine the headlines: "Jury Adjourns in Ray Trial Without Deliberating. Lawyers

Puzzled." But the judge *did* say we were in charge of the deliberation process, so if they didn't like it, too bad.

I drove home toward the bright afternoon sun and then became stuck in unusually heavy traffic. As I moved the car forward a few yards at a time, the magnitude of what I was facing began to sink in. I would lead a group of people searching for a unanimous decision. Eleven people would come in to court the next morning, sit down, and look my way expectantly. I felt old familiar fears rise inside me. Fear of making a mistake. Fear of making the wrong decision. I gripped the steering wheel tightly.

Maybe I should pray, I thought to myself.

This was strange. I didn't pray anymore, aside from the panicky utterances on airplanes I made since the turbulent flight from Salt Lake City had rattled me so badly. I was feeling the same way now, rattled and out of control. So right there in my car, I prayed. I prayed to a God that I believed had betrayed me after a life of righteousness and service to His church. A God that I had wished I had kept at a distance. It was a prayer born of desperation. "Please, God, whatever the verdict is, just please, don't let me fail."

◆　◆　◆

I had always been afraid of failure, ever since that day as a ten-year-old boy when I saw in church what can happen to the father of a failed son. I resolved to be the ideal Christian boy so I would not fail. This fear established a pattern for my life, making it difficult and sometimes impossible to make any decision or take any risk.

When I was eleven, I played in a youth soccer league. During a game, I tried to pass the ball across the field deep in our own side. The other team intercepted it for an easy score. I was embarrassed as I saw my teammates throw their hands up in frustration.

"What were you thinking?" our goalkeeper yelled at me.

After the game, I begged my mom to let me off the team. But she wouldn't hear of it, insisting I needed the exercise and fresh air.

Okay then, I thought to myself, but I won't try to pass the ball again.

I therefore adopted a playing style that could be described as "orbiting around the action." I never did anything other than run up and down the field and occupy space, but I didn't make a mistake either. During a practice session, the coach called me over to the sideline. The coach was a tall man with thick, black, curly hair and an enormous mustache across his face. He was a former professional soccer player and still dressed the part, complete with jersey, shorts, and white socks pulled up to his knees.

Coach knelt on one knee, so he was right at eye level with me. "Carl, do you believe in Jesus?"

The question surprised me. What did Jesus have to do with this? I thought coach would yell at me or tell me to hustle, not give me a Bible lesson.

I looked down at his white socks. "Uh, yes."

"Well you know what I think?" He waited for me to look up at him. "I think if Jesus Christ were on that field, he would try harder than any other player out there." Then his voice escalated into a shout. "Jesus would go for it! He would try to make a play and he wouldn't worry about it. NOW GET ON OUT THERE AND MAKE JESUS PROUD!"

I ran back onto the field, glad to be done with the sideline sermon. For the next game, I tried to play more like I supposed Jesus would have, and I made an extra play or two, to the oversized encouragement of the coach. But the inspiration didn't stick. I was still too terrified of mistakes.

Jesus would have been a perfect soccer player. I was a mere mortal, and I didn't come back to the team the following season. The fear of a wrong choice stayed with me for the rest of my life. I took forever

to make a decision, usually hoping a decision would happen by default so I couldn't be blamed for the outcome.

◆ ◆ ◆

Painfully aware that I suck at making decisions, I arrived the morning
of Tuesday, May 5, for the first day of deliberations and decision making. We normally parked our cars in the regular courthouse lot, next
to attorneys, members of the media, or even witnesses in the case.
Now the judge worried that we might be harassed or even threatened
since we were now in deliberations. He told us to park in a restricted
lot for the Sheriff's department. Deputies walked with us in and out of
the building to keep the press, or anyone else, away. This new escort
at times made me feel like a celebrity. How many people get a body-
guard to take them to work? Mostly, though, it worried me, knowing
that being a juror was a dangerous occupation. Truth be told, I wondered about my safety.

The very first witness in the case was visibly shaking testifying
before the accused witness killer.

The soldier flown in from Iraq testified he wanted nothing to do
with this trial out of fear for his own life.

Another witness testified that he was even threatened by Robert
Ray in the very parking lot we normally used.

I never received a threat, veiled or obvious. The defendant had
not so much as even looked at me crossly. Yet I couldn't help but feel
nervous as an armed guard brought me into the courthouse.

The jury room was more cramped than usual. All the exhibits
from trial were moved into the room so we could examine them: the
car door, the victim mannequins, sealed bags of clothing and bullets,
crime scene maps, and even some guns found in Robert Ray's car
(these were not the murder weapons, and they had been disabled). On
the table sat boxes of photographs and transcripts of interviews and
prison phone calls.

The one thing we couldn't have was the official transcript of the trial, where every word was captured by stenographers in the official record. The official record would have been immensely useful. For reasons I never understood, we had to rely solely on memory and any notes we had taken.

We surrendered our phones again to the bailiff because communication with the outside world was not allowed during deliberations. He collected the phones in a basket and in return gave me the two-way radio I would use to contact him. All that was missing was a bright red sign on the door that said QUARANTINED.

The bailiff left us. The door closed, and quiet descended. I could hear the small refrigerator buzzing in the corner of the room as everyone waited for me to say something. For a moment, the thought of getting on board an airliner flashed through my mind. The door was closed and locked, and there was nothing that could be done now except hope for a smooth flight. I thought of turbulence and being out of control. I tried to take a deep breath.

Getting to the bottom of all the charges would be a herculean task. The prosecution charged Ray with fourteen crimes, including illegal distribution of a controlled substance, bribing witnesses, intimidating witnesses, conspiracy to commit first-degree murder, and of course two counts of first-degree murder. The first charge we considered, selling drugs, was easy. The evidence was overwhelming. It only took us a few minutes to deliberate and unanimously vote guilty. Then the work became much more difficult.

Somehow, through the magic of jury selection, we had eleven other people who were stricken with the same fear of decisions and mistakes that I was. We took up an intimidation charge and discussed it for about an hour. We spread our notes on the table and wrote key points on a flip chart. After an hour, I decided to take a straw vote to see where we stood. None of us voted for guilty, and none of us voted for not guilty. Apparently, we were looking for someone to take the lead and make a decision. I asked for the jurors to share their thoughts, and I began to hear some common refrains.

"I don't know where to begin."

"I'm not sure what I think."

For my part, I didn't know what to think either, and I was the leader. I could empathize with the hesitancy on the part of everyone to be the first to offer an idea or an opinion. The dreaded words of *deadlock* and *failure* crept back into my mind as we left to get lunch from the courthouse cafeteria. We had reached lunchtime, and we had made no progress.

When we returned from lunch, I listed the legal components of the intimidation charge on the easel pad, and we began to discuss the evidence, or lack thereof, for each component. I decided to take another straw vote. This time, three jurors believed Robert Ray was guilty of intimidation. The rest were still undecided. We continued the discussion, poring over the same notes and evidence we had before. Then another vote, this time with a few more, including me, voting guilty. There were still undecided votes, maybe two or three by that point, but there were none for not guilty.

I voted guilty on the charge because I believed the evidence proved it beyond a reasonable doubt. Still, I voted with reluctance—the same reluctance I had when making any decision. This was now beyond testimony or discussions. This had moved from the realm of possibility to the realm of reality. I was making a decision, one that had very real consequences.

We had been in the jury room for a few hours discussing the intimidation charge when Greg announced that he needed a cigarette break. Since we had to stay together, we all went with Greg to the smoking area, a small patio outside the cafeteria that was enclosed by a ten-foot brick wall. We sat on the patio furniture while Greg smoked a few feet away in the corner. I looked up at the sky and saw a passenger jet fly overhead, leaving a brilliant white contrail across the clear blue. I watched it until it disappeared from view, on the other side of the brick wall, another reminder that we were trapped and an omen, I thought, that turbulence was ahead.

I could sense this same trepidation in my fellow jurors as our first day of deliberations dragged on. Even if they did make a decision and voted on the intimidation charge, they did so with a sigh, leaning back and slumping against their chairs unhappily, hands rubbing their foreheads like they were trying to massage away a headache. Committing to a verdict was not easy.

We marked our jury forms with an "x" in the box for "guilty" and signed our names. This felt morbidly final to me. What if we somehow got it wrong? What if we missed something important? When we reached four o'clock in the afternoon, we had eleven votes for "guilty" on the first intimidation charge. The lone undecided vote was Kelly. She leaned back in her chair with arms crossed and a scowl on her face.

"What do you need?" I asked.

Kelly stared out the window and didn't look my way in response. "I don't know what I need." Her voice was flat.

Vicki spoke next. "We've been talking about this for hours—all afternoon. There's really nothing new we can discuss."

Kelly continued staring out the window, unmoved.

"Do you think he is guilty?" Again, Kelly did not reply, her gaze still fixed out the window.

Vicki did not relent. "Well, what about not guilty? Do you think he is not guilty?"

"I don't think he is not guilty." Kelly suddenly turned and faced Vicki. Her eyes narrowed.

"Well then, what's the problem?" Vicki matched Kelly's stare. "Why won't you vote guilty?"

"I don't know." Kelly's voice softened, and she looked down at the table. She tapped the table leg gently with her foot a few times.

After a pause, Vicki opened her notebook. "Well, let me explain why I voted for guilty. Maybe it will help you."

There was something about the way Vicki said this—*maybe it will help you*—that ignited an anger in Kelly. Kelly and Vicki were in very different places in life. Kelly was a young newlywed, not far from her college soccer days. Vicki was divorced and struggling to make ends meet for her and her teenage daughter. Stuck on jury duty, Vicki had lost the income from her receptionist job. The stress of all of this drove her to take up smoking after she had quit just the year before. She bummed cigarettes from Greg on the patio.

Vicki kept explaining all the key points in her decision, very self-assured despite Kelly's stare from across the table.

"Shut up, shut up!" Kelly abruptly slapped both her hands on the table and glared at Vicki. Several other jurors flinched.

"No!" Vicki stood up, her chair pushed back into the wall. "I have a right to state my opinions. Don't I?" Vicki turned and looked right at me.

"Uh…"

"I don't care what you think." Kelly leaned into the table. "I don't care what any of you think."

The other jurors looked down and shifted in their chairs. This was exactly what I was afraid of—going out of control. The room suddenly felt stifling hot, and I wanted to yank the door open and run to some cooler air. Kelly and Vicki started to talk over each other.

"You have no right to…"

"If you would only listen…"

Suddenly, Kelly ripped the verdict form from her notebook. She angrily circled the "guilty" box over and over and then signed her name with an exaggerated flourish of her pen. Vicki was still talking. Kelly picked up the jury form and held it up for all to see. She pointed at the word "guilty" and then slapped the paper onto the table. Vicki stopped talking. We all held our breath for a moment.

"I just wanted to explain..." Vicki's voice trailed off. Kelly glared at her, her mouth tightly shut.

"Okay." I stood up, trying to break up the action, adding to my ineffective "Uh..." from a minute before. "Things got a little heated there, but we don't have to rush things. Let's just slow down. One voice at a time. Vicki, what is it you wanted to say?"

"Nothing. Apparently, I've been told to shut up." Vicki pulled her chair up from behind her and sat. Tears welled in her eyes.

I looked toward Kelly. "Do you need anything else? Should we talk about this more or maybe revisit this tomorrow?"

Without looking at me, Kelly pushed her verdict form across the table. The page flew up in the air and fluttered down in front of me.

The decision was finally unanimous. We had taken almost the entire day to decide only one of the charges. But nobody felt good about having reached a decision. We still had twelve more charges to go, including the two most serious ones.

Will we ever get through this?

To make matters worse, we ended the day with two jurors fighting.

I decided we had enough for the day. I called for the bailiff on the two-way radio, so we could be dismissed and escorted back to our cars. I tried to catch Kelly's attention as she got up to leave. I wanted to talk to her, to make sure she was going to be all right. But she bolted for the door, staring straight ahead, her lips pressed tight. Vicki sat in her chair, crying softly.

Lois, the retired school principal, reached over the table and placed her hand on Vicki's arm. "Don't take it personally. This is hard for all of us and some of us just don't want to make a decision."

I walked with my deputy escort to my car. I drove home and sat in the garage, feeling disappointed with myself for how the day had ended. We had made it through only one day of deliberations and already I was exhausted. I wondered if I had the ability to do this job of judgment. This was a lonely task. I was not allowed to talk about any of this with anyone. Normally I preferred working alone. But now I wanted help. I wanted someone to put a hand on my shoulder and tell me I would get through this. We would be starting deliberations again only hours later in the morning, and there was nobody in the world who could help me.

I walked into the house. Maybe there would be something in there I could do successfully. Dishes, perhaps. There's no way I could screw up the dishes.

◆　◆　◆

I grew up in a church that believed God was manifested in the Trinity: God the Father, God the Son, and God the Holy Spirit. God the Father was the creator of the universe and of life itself. He was perfect in every way. His Son was Jesus, sent to Earth to redeem humankind from its sin, sin that offended the perfect nature of God. The Holy Spirit was a far more nebulous concept. Our church believed the Holy Spirit was an active force in the world, moving among the believers and filling them with spiritual power. Sometimes this power took the form of quiet inspiration. Other times it was charismatic and public, revealed in the speaking of tongues, words of wisdom, or healing. Each evangelical church might vary in how they believed the Holy Spirit works, but one thing was constant—God's spirit was manifested in the hearts of the believers.

Because I was the "ideal" Christian boy, people naturally assumed that I was filled with God's spirit. At times, I had tried to speak in tongues, the so-called "baptism of the Holy Spirit." But I was never sure that I wasn't just babbling along with the same speech patterns I had heard from other tongues-speakers. The reality was I never really felt anything spiritual or supernatural. No power. No joy. No inspiration.

This was one of the great ironies of my Christian life. I was so good at being a Christian, and such a wonderful example, that people would look at me and remark that I was led by the Spirit, full of God's power. The apparent proof of it was there in my righteous living—showing the world an example of Biblical knowledge, service to others, and moral purity. I spoke publicly on moral and conservative political issues with power and authority. But I harbored a secret.

Inside, I didn't experience anything I could discern as being from God. No burning power. No inspired visions. Nothing I would consider exuberant. As I got older and struggled with my marriage, what I felt from God more than anything was betrayal. If there was a Holy Spirit, it wasn't active in my life. Most non-Christians had more spirit than I did.

After only a day of trying to lead eleven others through deliberations and decision making, I wanted something from the Holy Spirit. Inspiration. Power. Confidence. Anything, really. Anything to replace the desperation growing in me.

◆ ◆ ◆

We filed into our room for day two of deliberations amid small talk about the weather, the crowds in the lobby downstairs, and the latest sports scores. As we settled into our chairs, the room became quiet. I knew as the foreperson I was supposed to do something or say something to get us started again. But it was Kelly who broke the silence.

"Can I just say something?"

"Sure," I said. "Go right ahead."

Kelly looked down toward the table, rocking back and forth ever so slightly in her chair. Her lower lip trembled, and she closed her eyes. Tears pooled under her eyelids. Then she shook with sobs. As the tears flowed down her face, she bowed her head nearly to the table. Her long, blond hair slid smoothly from her shoulders, and covered her face.

"I just can't do this." Her voice was strained, a high pitch. "I just can't put away a man like this. Why was I chosen to do this?" That was all she could blurt out before her sobs once again took over, and she covered her face with her hands.

And there, after months of replaying my vision again and again in my mind, it was now being played out live before me. She even said the very words I had heard months before.

I just can't do this.

Normally, someone crying uncontrollably would be stressful for me, if not completely panic-inducing. I sat many times on our green leather couch, paralyzed with fear and indecision as my wife broke down in tears bemoaning her lonely marriage. Normally, I would sit perplexed and trying desperately to think of something to say. I would brace myself for her to look up through a tear stained face and say, "I want a divorce."

That day, there in the jury room, was different. I had seen this coming in my vision, and somehow that made me feel calmer. A thought, a voice, something, spoke to me in my mind.

You don't need to say anything. You don't need to fear anything. You just need to wait.

I was feeling a power inside me that I had never felt before. It was spiritual, filling, calming. Was it God? Was God's spirit finally falling on me, not in a church or in the midst of performing some great religious deed, but in the middle of a gruesome murder trial?

Marie, the hotel manager, slid her chair close to Kelly and placed a box of tissues on the table in front of her. "Oh honey, you are not alone. We are all feeling overwhelmed by this."

"It's just moving so fast." Kelly was trying to gain control of her breath and voice. "I'm just not ready for this. I want to go back and start over. This is a man's life we are dealing with."

"This isn't easy for me, either." Rebecca, the payroll clerk, spoke next, her eyes filling with tears. "I think we are all feeling what you are feeling."

I said nothing, nor did I feel the need to speak up. A thought came into my mind—You are not doing this job alone. I just sat and watched as each juror spoke up, confessing how they were feeling. We were all afraid.

There is much to fear when deciding if another human being is guilty of a crime. When I saw a criminal face justice in the news or in the storyline of a movie, I felt satisfied seeing the bad guy get what was coming to him. It was often, dare I say it, *entertaining*. In real life, we can't leave the story behind in the theater or change the channel in search of the next amusement. We would think about this decision the rest of our lives. I imagined that even years removed from the trial, I might hear about some evidence that wasn't allowed to be shown in court that would have changed my decision. Or I would learn I just plain got it wrong.

No matter how we decided, half of those involved would be devastated. We would be forced to sit and watch as half the people reacted in anger, grief, and frustration. I imagined that there would be outbursts of emotion, and people would look at me with hate for what I had decided. This would be true whether we voted guilty or not guilty. I expected this reality to make me feel heavy and sad, like the trite saying, "a weight on my shoulders." Instead, I felt empty and light, nervous and twitchy. The day before, our first day of deliberations, my leg shook with nervous energy under the conference table, vibrating with enough force to ripple the water in my glass. It was on days like that when I could not suppress a yell as I sat in my car to drive home.

Now though, as Kelly cried before all of us, I did not feel light, like my nervous energy might throw me out of my chair. Instead, I felt *solid*. Kelly pushed herself upright and her sobs eased.

"I'm sorry." Her voice was calm again. She dabbed at her eyes with the tissues. "I'm sorry, but I just needed to say that, to get it off my chest. I don't want to be here. I don't want to do this. But since I have no choice, can we at least start over?"

"No, *I'm* sorry," I said. "I brought this on us. I was the one pushing constantly for votes. I think the constant voting put too much pressure on us and made it hard for people who wanted to talk more. It pits us against each other." I was admitting failure, but surprisingly I felt stronger for it, not weaker.

"You didn't do anything wrong, Carl." Marie wiped the tears off her face with a tissue. "You've never done this before either, and Kelly was just expressing how we feel. This is a lot of pressure."

"Then let's change things," I said. "Forget about what we are going to do first, second, third. No more straw votes. We will talk and work together before we take any votes. I won't even mention voting until I sense we are ready. I just want all of us to follow three rules in here."

Normally, if I am going to speak to a group of people, or think I might have to speak to a group of people, I prepare and try to find the right words well ahead of time, so I can rehearse. But that day in the jury room, I was not prepared. Each word I was saying was unrehearsed, spontaneous.

I told the jurors that we should follow three principles for how we would work together:

One step at a time. We can't allow ourselves to think about what is coming next. Stay focused on the decision at hand.

Follow the law. The judge already gave us instructions. That is all we need to follow. We don't have to worry about what anyone else thinks we should do.

Have courage. If you feel lost or confused, or you just don't like the way something is going, speak out, even if you are the only one.

Where did this come from? I wondered for a moment. Is this what is feels like to be inspired?

"You're the leader, Carl." The voice came from somewhere near Greg's end of the table. "Just keep us on track."

"I feel better about this already." Another voice.

"I just want to say that we are only going to get through this together, as a team."

What an amazing feeling, I thought, that after I had felt so helpless, now I could feel affirmed.

"I'd like to make one more suggestion," I continued. "The murder charges. They are hanging over our heads and have been since we started. We should deal with those now. Let's tackle the tough charges first, and once we do, the rest will fall into place. Let's take a quick break, and then get back to work."

As everyone stood up and headed for the restrooms or coffee machine, I approached Kelly.

"About yesterday, I just want to say..."

"Water under the bridge." Kelly said, looking at me. Her eyes were red, but her face was calm again.

What happened next was markedly different from the previous day. Instead of sitting back and seeing how each of us would vote, we started a lively discussion, sorting out each aspect of a charge and what we thought the evidence showed for each. Instead of reviewing our notes on our own, we were opening up the evidence boxes and laying things out on the table. People began to jump up and start outlining their thoughts on the easel pad. And what was most different from the day before was that our discussions were moving quickly. We had a new courage to confront the tough decisions. As I gave up control, courage followed. I *wanted* help, perhaps for the first time in my life. And help came.

◆　◆　◆

I could write a separate book about everything that happened during our deliberations and all the evidence we considered. We had seen hundreds of exhibits and four weeks of testimony from dozens of witnesses. To understand how we reached our decision, it is necessary to summarize some key evidence.

There was no question that Robert Ray didn't pull the trigger. He wasn't even at the scene of the shooting. This meant I had to decide if he was the one who ordered the killing and ensured that it would happen—what is known in legal terms as "aiding and abetting." This is just as serious in the eyes of the law as the crime itself.

To successfully convince others to carry out a murder on his behalf, Robert Ray needed to have influence. And he certainly did. He was definitely the boss. He controlled the details of the entire drug dealing business. We heard testimony that Sir Mario Owens idolized Robert since their days together at Overland High School in Aurora. Owens would do anything to stay in Robert's good graces. Owens was tried and convicted for his role in the murders of Javad and Vivian the year before Robert Ray's trial. The jury was convinced that Owens was the one in the maroon car who emptied two guns into Javad's car. We also heard testimony from Robert's family about the consequences of disobeying his wishes, which included the loss of money that he paid the family members each month. Robert's family was completely dependent on him financially.

Robert was also smart and did not attract attention. He kept a low profile, choosing to live in a modest townhome, and drove average, non-descript, used cars. He was clean-cut and polite, blending in with his neighbors. He did not use drugs himself, calling drug users "suckers." He rarely drank alcohol, not liking how he felt out-of-control when drunk—like he was at Lowry Park on the night that started this entire mess. I came to view Robert Ray as a smart man who was attentive to detail. He would have no problem organizing a plot and getting others to do the dirty work.

Robert's control of his enterprise was rewarding. By some accounts, he was making $40,000 per month using two other businesses as fronts. He knew what would happen should he ever get caught and jailed. He knew because he saw it happen to his brothers when they were jailed on various drug charges—someone else would step in and take the business and he would never be able to regain it. The charges he faced in the Gregory Vann case—accessory to murder—only carried only a six-year prison sentence. Still, he couldn't afford the risk of even a six-year sentence. He had the most to lose.

After the murder of Gregory Vann at Lowry Park, the police had no knowledge of Sir Mario Owens. Robert knew this. That is why he kept Owens out of view, telling him to stay away from court hearings. Not even Javad had identified Sir Mario Owens—he was only going to testify that he saw Robert Ray at Lowry Park when Greg Vann was shot and killed. Robert knew this, too, from the evidentiary hearings done by his attorney. If Owens had decided to leave Robert Ray and move away from Colorado for good, it is likely he would have escaped prosecution entirely. Sir Mario Owens had nothing to gain from killing Javad except favor with Robert Ray.

Robert's motive and Owen's loyalty were key evidence. There was other evidence, too. Robert asked several people to offer Javad money for skipping out on his testimony. When that failed, he offered to pay the money to whoever would "take Javad out." He asked still others, including his wife, to make contact with Javad and deliver threatening messages. Robert had also managed to get another witness to skip out on his testimony. He did that with one confrontation in the courthouse parking lot. Everyone knew how Robert felt about snitches.

"Snitches die," he once told his wife, "those ho'-ass niggas."

I just didn't believe that anyone else had the same motive to want Javad dead. It was Robert Ray alone who would benefit. He had the willing posse to help him, and his crew knew he was expecting results.

On the night of the murders, Robert was with several friends and family members at the house of his stepfather. They were hanging out doing nothing in particular when Robert's phone "chirped" announcing an incoming message. It was a combination cell phone and two-way radio. It was faster to communicate over the two-way, since it didn't require dialing and waiting for an answer. Sir Mario Owens had one of these phones as well. When a message came in on the two-way radio, it played over the speaker, so anyone nearby could hear it. That is why everyone in the house heard the unmistakable Louisiana drawl of Sir Mario Owens.

"It's tooken' care of."

Robert didn't reply. Instead, he turned the television to the evening news. Everyone in the house fell silent as they watched the breaking coverage of a shooting in Aurora. The reports showed the pictures of Javad's gold-colored Chevrolet Monte Carlo, pockmarked with bullet holes. They knew—everyone in that house knew—why this happened. Many of them had been following that gold car around for the previous week.

But there was one question the defense raised above all else: did Robert Ray actually tell Sir Mario Owens to kill Javad? Not scare him or intimidate him, but actually *kill* him. The defense team, in their closing arguments, said that Owens acted completely on his own. I didn't believe that. But then the defense attorney said something interesting. He stated that maybe the gunshots were meant to scare Javad, and not to kill him.

This statement made me pause. I believed that Owens only shot at Javad because Robert asked him to. Robert had clearly been in the lead when it came to the efforts to prevent Javad's testimony, but maybe he never wanted Javad dead. Maybe the gunfire was just one last attempt to really scare Javad, an attempt that went horribly wrong.

This last thought, that maybe Robert didn't really want Javad dead, kept me and most of the others on the jury from voting "guilty" right away. This was a seductive argument presented by the defense that offered a way out for anyone who was having doubts. Sir Mario Owens was already on death row for the murders. If a juror was not convinced beyond a reasonable doubt that Robert Ray gave the order to kill, that juror could vote not guilty and still be assured that someone would be punished for the crime.

We adjourned after day two with this thought waiting for our return: did Robert order a kill or just a scare? As I walked back to my car with my deputy escort, I wondered if we would be able to overcome this one last argument, or if this meant we would find Robert Ray not guilty of first-degree murder.

◆　◆　◆

"We should take a pulse-check and see where everyone is at." This is how I started our third day of deliberations. I wanted to have everyone tell the group what they were thinking—if they had made a decision, and if not, what they would like to discuss further. I wasn't expecting much to happen. I thought we would be deliberating for at least a couple more days.

"Who would like to go first?" I asked.

I glanced around the room. Most everyone sat still, hands in laps, staring down at the center of the table. I looked to my left toward Greg, who was sitting at the head of the table, slouched down in his chair, his elbow on the armrest with his hand propping up his chin.

Greg was staring at the car door—Javad's car door—that was leaning against the wall. He didn't appear to move or even blink. I couldn't tell if he was even breathing.

"Greg, you look deep in thought. What's going through your mind?"

A few seconds went by before he shifted in his chair, pushing himself upright. He swiveled the chair back and forth uneasily, but never looked up at the rest of us. Greg was one of the quieter people on our jury. He rarely spoke during deliberations unless it was "his turn" or someone asked him a direct question. When he did speak, he was very concise.

"It's this car door." Greg was still staring at the door. "All those bullet holes in such a small space." He stood up and bent over the car door, touching each bullet hole as he counted them. "One, two, three, four, five, six, seven, eight, nine, ten, eleven, twelve." He sat back down in his chair heavily, still looking at the door. "Twelve." He shook his head slowly several times. "Man, that is not what you do when you want to scare someone. I mean, if you wanted to scare him, you would maybe fire a shot or two into the tires or maybe a rear window. But this...this is what you do when you want to kill."

Greg slumped back into his seat again, resting his chin in his hand, still staring at the car door. Once again, the room became quiet. Everyone seemed to breathe more quietly, not wanting to make a sound. I rotated my chair around to look at the car door, which was almost directly behind me. As I looked at it, a felt a nervous twitch in my gut, like I had just stumbled unexpectedly across a horrifying site.

Holy shit, I thought to myself. The words caught me by surprise. I couldn't believe I had not noticed this before. I held up my notebook and it covered most of the bullet holes. It was an immense amount of firepower concentrated in such a small space.

Out of the corner of my eye, I saw Lois, the retired principal, pop upright into her chair.

"I think Greg is right." Her voice was loud and clear. "You just don't shoot like that unless you want him dead."

I turned my chair back around and saw James, who sat directly across the table from me. James was a tall and athletic man. In his college days, some twenty-five years before, he played football on a nationally-ranked team. Football is a tough guy sport. That is why what happened next surprised me.

James stared up and ahead, like he could see the sky above the wall behind me. He took a shallow breath. Then his lips began to quiver, and suddenly he was awash in tears. "Oh my god," he stammered through his tears. "He did it."

James was openly sobbing now. He covered his face with his hands, yet the tears still flowed, now down the side of his face onto his neck. He tried to regain some steady breathing, which took him about thirty seconds. Several others started to cry as well.

James finally calmed himself and wiped his face on the sleeve of his shirt. Then he resumed looking up and ahead like he had before. "He did it. He wanted Javad dead and he killed those two young people. And for what?" Now the tears started again as James covered his eyes with his hands.

With that, James became the first one of us to say out loud that Robert Ray was guilty. I had been afraid to say this myself, even as the evidence made the decision clear. I didn't want to be wrong. And as the foreperson, I felt like I should not push my own view but let the group arrive at their conclusion first. But now, I took my own advice. One step at a time. Have courage.

"Yes," I said aloud. "Robert Ray is guilty. He told Sir Mario Owens to take care of the problem, and it is clear to me now that he wanted Javad dead."

There. I did it. I said it. I decided.

This brought no relief from the pressure of the decision, like I had wanted. Instead, I felt incredibly sad. Uncontrollably sad. I began to cry. I almost never cried. The last time might have been in 1992 when my mother died. Even then, I somehow held back the tears in my eyes and kept them from rolling onto my face. Crying, especially when someone could see me, made me feel vulnerable and out of control. That day, in the jury room with eleven others looking on, I did something I had never done before. I let the tears flow down my face unabated. I made no effort to wipe them away or to hide my face. I didn't care who saw me. I didn't care what anyone thought. I didn't care that I felt out of control. The tears splashed onto my notebook.

The two biggest men in the room, James and I, were now the leaders of a crying session. There was no wailing or loud outbursts. Just quiet tears from each juror as they in turn stated how they felt: Robert Ray was responsible for the murder of two promising young people.

He killed a witness to protect his empire and evade prosecution for a charge that was trivial in comparison to murder. As I thought about this and listened to what the other jurors were saying, I felt pain, loss, grief, anger, and sadness. There was no holding it back now because I didn't want to hold it back. The emotions—yes, there were emotions at last—flooded in, and I sat and.let them wash over me in a cramped and stifling jury room.

Whatever fear or doubt about making the big decision dissolved in each of us at that moment. The dam had broken. I felt a connection to the eleven others who were with me. I was proud of them—proud of their courage. We made our decision even though we knew it was going to cost us. We would now have to deal with punishment of the crime which meant another month in court for another trial and another set of deliberations.

But this time, it would be even more difficult. We would have to decide if Robert Ray would spend the rest of his life in prison or be sentenced to die. And we would have to live with that decision forever.

◆　◆　◆

After the emotion that started our third day of deliberations, I decided we needed a break to regain composure and settle down. When we returned, it was time to take a formal vote. As we sat at the table, I asked each juror two questions. First, do you want more time to discuss anything about the murder charges? If the answer was no, then I asked the second question. Have you decided your verdict? Each juror said they were ready to vote.

On the charge of murder in the first degree of Javad Marshall Fields, we found the defendant guilty.

On the charge of murder in the first degree of Vivian Wolfe, we found the defendant guilty.

The rest of the charges fell into place from there. We decided

Robert Ray was guilty of eleven of the fourteen charges—the three not guilty verdicts were on various intimidation charges of his family. By the middle of the third day, we were done.

As was becoming my habit, I gave all the verdict forms to Rebecca, the payroll clerk, for her to double-check. When that was done, I signed the official verdict forms and then picked up the two-way radio to call the bailiff.

Lunch was brought in for us from the courthouse cafeteria, so we wouldn't have to leave the room. We ate and watched from our second-story window as the parking lot of the courthouse began to fill with cars. News vans from all the local television stations were parked along the sidewalk. The TV crews frantically set up cameras while reporters looked into handheld mirrors and smoothed their hair. The defense lawyers arrived and walked briskly across the parking lot. Family members of Javad and Vivian strode to the door, holding hands.

"Wow, all this because of us!" James said as he took a bite of his sandwich.

"I know, we've really done it now!" Greg laughed at his own reply.

"I promise I'm not going to cry in the courtroom." James was smiling broadly.

Another half-hour later, there was a knock at the door, and the bailiff appeared. "They are ready for you now."

We lined up by juror number in the hallway and marched single-file into the courtroom. We were surprised to see the alternate jurors waiting for us, already seated in the jury box. They had been shut in a different room for the past three days, watching movies and reading books, on stand-by in case one of us could not continue deliberations for some reason.

The courtroom was packed with people standing along the walls and in the back. I sat in chair twelve and looked up at the judge to find he was already looking at me.

"Juror twelve, I understand you are the foreperson. Is this true?"

I swallowed hard. *How did he know it was me? Oh great, now everyone knows it's me.*

"Yes, sir." Then I remembered from all the Hollywood courtroom dramas I had seen that I was supposed to say, "your honor" and not "sir."

"The bailiff tells me you have reached a unanimous verdict on all fourteen counts. Is that true?"

"Yes, your honor." I got it right the second time.

The bailiff came over to me and I handed him the verdict forms. He took them to the judge. The judge then examined each one as the courtroom sat in complete silence. No squeaking of chairs. No clearing of throats. People seemed to be holding their breath. We could hear the sound of each page being turned by the judge as he read the pages without any visible reaction.

Then he began to read each verdict out loud. I looked at the prosecutors. The three of them sat close together at their table along with the lead detective in the case. Years of hard work, thousands of pages of legal briefs, dozens of evidentiary hearings, and hundreds of interviews came down to this moment. The detective had her elbows on the table, hands clasped as if in prayer. She rested her forehead on her hands and closed her eyes. As each verdict was read, she took another breath and held it, waiting for the next verdict.

When the judge announced the murder verdicts, I could hear some soft crying coming from the front row of the gallery, where the families of Javad and Vivian sat. I was surprised that there was no other noise at all. Only later would I find out that the judge had given everyone a stern warning of very dire consequences if there were any outbursts in his courtroom. There were no theatrics. It was a matter-of-fact presentation. The lead defense attorney then stood and somberly asked the judge for a jury confirmation. The judge asked each of us the same question, "Is this and was this your verdict?"

Each of us in turn said yes. The judge then explained to us that we would return the next Monday to start a new trial, this one to determine the punishment. Everyone stood as we exited the courtroom.

The bailiff advised us to stay put until the hubbub of the news reports and the parking lot traffic had quieted down. This gave us some time together as a jury again, now with a big milestone behind us. There were hugs and a few more tears. I thanked each juror and told them not to worry about what would come next.

The ladies hugged me, the men gave me a firm handshake and a pat on the shoulder. "You got us through this," they told me. "We are so lucky you are here."

Whenever I had finished a big task at school or work or gave a presentation on stage, I wanted immediate feedback. If I didn't get that feedback, I felt tense, sick to my stomach, twitchy. I could think of nothing else until the grades were in.

But this time, after the verdict, I didn't feel the need to say anything at all. No summary. No lessons to heed next time. I just stood there in the jury room, my hands in my pockets, posture relaxed, watching everyone around me talk, hug, cry. I was more satisfied with the last three days in the jury room than any other performance of my life. I had made a big decision and led eleven others through the ordeal. We had overcome adversity together.

eleven
THE CIRCLE

The South Side of Chicago was infamous for decades because of its many public housing projects. These places became so full of drugs, crime, and irredeemable poverty, the city housing authority eventually declared the projects were hopeless. They decided to spread residents out in regular neighborhoods instead of keeping them together in large buildings. The projects have since been demolished to make way for mixed-income housing developments available on the open market. But the names of the projects live on in Chicago lore, especially the Robert Taylor homes and Ida B. Wells homes.

Wedged between these housing projects sat a group of two-story, tan brick buildings. These apartments were arranged in a semicircle, with a section of lawn in front of them, a rarity in the concrete landscape of the city. The lawn was shaped in a semicircle as well. On a map, the entire housing development, apartments and lawn combined, formed a circle, and that is what residents called it. The Circle was one of the childhood homes of Robert Ray, and it became the centerpiece of his mitigation evidence.

Mitigating circumstances are evidence a jury considers when deciding the appropriate punishment for a crime. They are reasons presented by the defense team—reasons why a juror might choose a lesser punishment. In Robert Ray's case, the choice was between the death penalty and life in prison without parole. By Colorado law, a decision for the death penalty must be unanimous. If even one juror voted no, the punishment would default to life in prison. The defense team, then, needed only to convince one person on my jury there were enough mitigating circumstances to spare Robert Ray's life. They spent two weeks trying to do just that. Exhibit one was the place Robert Ray was raised: The Circle.

◆　◆　◆

Much of my childhood was in Laporte, a small town in Northern Colorado just outside Fort Collins, about seventy miles north of Denver. After my father's career in the Air Force, we moved to a ten-acre farm nestled against the foothills of the Rockies. Even though my dad had no agricultural training or background, he started a chicken hatchery business, investing his savings to get it started. After flying fighter jets in the Vietnam War, shooting down enemy aircraft and making dozens of bombing runs, the idea of a quiet life of farm work and living off the land was enticing to my father. There would be no hectic big city or urban living for us.

We used the land to raise a variety of small livestock in addition to the chickens: goats, sheep, rabbits, ducks, and turkeys. My mother tended a large garden that included a dozen tomato plants, rows of vegetables, potatoes, and a half-acre of corn. We had apple trees on the property, and I would often climb them in the late summer, pick an apple, and eat it, often while still clinging to the branches. The apples were small and had a powerful tartness with just enough sweetness to persuade me into taking another bite.

Each autumn brought a busy time of harvesting, canning, and storing our produce in a 1950s-era bomb shelter that we converted into a cool, damp and dark cellar. We spent hours cutting apples into slices and running them through a dehydrator to turn them into dense, chewy chunks that could be stored for months. For the corn, we sliced it off the cob and packed it into rows of cans neatly stacked in the cellar. My mom would cook the tomatoes and potatoes into stews that she stored in a large freezer in the garage. She was thrilled when we splurged on a wheat grinder, so she could make her own flour. We could be nearly self-sufficient, and that was a relief in the difficult economy of the early 1980s.

The chicken hatchery was busy, requiring all of us to pitch in and help as much as we could. Every Monday and Thursday, five thousand chicks would hatch in the small warehouse on our property. The air would fill with shrill peeping noises. Sometimes my two younger sisters and I would help sort the chickens by sex, gently dropping the squirming yellow chicks from the incubator trays into cardboard boxes for shipment to farms and poultry businesses across the Rocky Mountain area.

Every now and then a rebellious little chick would escape and scamper away and we would give chase. At first this new task was fun. The chicks were cute little fuzzy balls of yellow. They pecked inquisitively at our fingers. I gave names to the chicks that showed some character. But soon the sheer volume of the job overwhelmed us, and we learned to put aside the cuteness for clinical efficiency in sorting.

Monday and Thursday afternoons became a numbing mass of yellow feathers and never-ending peeping noise. Sometimes we would yell, "quiet!" as loudly as we could. The sudden noise would startle the chicks, and the din would pause for a few precious moments. Then after about ten seconds there would be a tentative "peep" from somewhere in the crowd. Another "peep" would answer back, and twenty seconds later, the throng of chicks would return to full volume.

Despite selling ten thousand chickens each week, the business was not profitable, and soon it had exhausted all my father's savings. After two years and a million chickens, he shut the business down and sold off the incubator. About the same time, he also took over our small church after the regular pastor resigned. This was yet another job for which he had no formal training, and it completed a rather unusual career trifecta. As my dad was fond of saying, he went "from fighter-plane jock to shepherd of the flock."

We became dependent on donations to the church for our income. That wasn't enough in the inflation-ravaged economy of the early 1980s. Most of the congregation had no extra money, and most families stopped giving altogether. My dad tried to fill the gap with odd jobs as he could find them, mowing lawns and remodeling basements. A large hailstorm one summer day damaged thousands of homes but was a blessing of work for him on a roofing crew. My mom sent him out in the heat each day with a cooler full of watermelon from our garden. I didn't know then we were on the verge of poverty. It seemed to me we had an abundance, especially of apples, potatoes, and corn. And yes, we had plenty of chickens.

Just outside our back fence, where the mountains met the plains, the land rose abruptly, covered by trees and topped by a rocky ridge. The area became my country playground. My cousins would visit often, and we would scamper over the back fence to the world beyond, toting slingshots and pockets full of smooth rocks for ammunition. The Cache La Poudre river flowed just a five-minute walk away, its shores covered in thick grass during the summer, the water cold with snowmelt from higher up in the mountains.

I remember the first time I cast a lure into the river. It landed with a small splash near the opposite bank and floated down with the current.

I tightened up the slack when the lure reached a deep eddy, the water a smooth brown color. Almost immediately, I felt a sharp tug on the line. A shot of adrenaline coursed from the fishing pole to my hands and down to my knees. I saw a flash of silver and green, and seconds later a fat rainbow trout was flopping at my feet in the grass. I held it up and admired it, the mossy green of its back contrasting with streaks of silver and pink on its sides and belly.

My birthday was only a week apart from one of my cousins. When I turned eleven, we shared a simple birthday party at our house. After cake and ice cream, we were out exploring again. We were in a dry irrigation canal when we came upon a faded and torn blue canvas duffel bag. Inside we found clothes, keys, a wallet, shoes, papers, and a knife. My cousin said we should leave it there and tell our parents what we found. Our parents were concerned enough to call the Sheriff's office, who sent a deputy to our house. The deputy drove us in his car to where we found the bag, just a few yards off the road.

After some investigation and calls back to dispatch, the deputy told us the bag belonged to a man who had been missing for many days. The items would be returned to the man's family. The deputy wished my cousin and I happy birthday and posed for a picture with us as we stood next to his car. I thought a lot about that bag in the following days. I wondered if the man was dead. It frightened me that I might have touched things belonging to a dead man. I wondered if ghosts were real and if I would now be haunted by this man for messing with his stuff.

As it turned out, I never saw any ghosts. My life had been free of any encounters with mortality until my mother died of cancer a decade later. I had never been held at gunpoint, never had to run for my life, or never even been in a serious accident. And my eleventh birthday had been the best ever: I got to ride in a real police car.

◆　◆　◆

Where Robert Ray was raised in the South Side of Chicago, a ride in a police car was not an adventure. The police, when they were present, were to be avoided, because Robert's older brothers dabbled in selling drugs. Young Robert was often used as a lookout, riding his bicycle up and down the sidewalks and signaling his brothers when he spotted a cop car.

Robert had two older brothers: Kevin, who, during the trial, was in jail on drug charges, and Kendrick, who, during the trial, was out on parole. Both brothers testified on behalf of Robert, Kevin appearing in his jail uniform. They told us that when they were growing up in Chicago, they started selling drugs as teenagers. Kevin and Kendrick cut and bundled marijuana in their house while little Robert would look on. Selling drugs was part of growing up and surviving for them, and this made the police the enemy.

As I heard this testimony, I imagined how ridiculous my birthday ride in a police car would have seemed to these three brothers. Playing outside for hours at a time in wide-open country would have been a perfect fairy tale to them. My childhood would have seemed right out of a Norman Rockwell painting or Andy Griffith's Mayberry, as we hopped over fences to explore acres of open space, slingshots in our back pockets.

By contrast, crossing boundaries on the South Side could mean a deadly encounter with a rival gang. Robert and his brothers learned as kids to stay on certain sidewalks and avoid crossing particular streets. A slingshot would be no match for the handguns that were the tools for drug dealers. Playtime was often cut short by violence. When the older kids or adults would see that a fight was imminent, usually between rival drug dealers, they would call out, "Get the shorties inside!" The younger kids knew this warning was directed at them, so they would scamper inside and crouch down behind furniture, away from the windows. Gunfire would then erupt. Maybe someone would be hurt or killed.

Kendrick told us that he and Robert had seen more than a few bodies lying in The Circle. For Robert, death could visit the neighborhood in the middle of playtime. The suggestion was obvious: growing up in such a place would make a person more accustomed to violence, and thus more likely to engage in it. According to the defense team, this wasn't an excuse for murder, but it should mitigate what punishment Robert might receive.

The defense team did more than pin their mitigation hopes on the idea that children raised in Chicago were conditioned to violence. They argued that Robert Ray also experienced head injuries when he was young, and those injuries damaged the key executive functions of his brain, diminishing his capacity to fully understand the consequences of his actions. Several internationally-recognized experts from prestigious universities and hospitals testified about brain development and criminal behavior. The jury became instant experts on the brain, critical thinking, and how a few hits to the head can affect a person.

But the physiological testimony was a side-show compared to stories about the South Side and the Circle. In a two-week period, Robert's defense team called at least two dozen other witnesses, and every one of them spoke about the violent life on Chicago's South Side, especially for young children. One witness, an expert in childhood trauma in war zones, compared Chicago to Bosnia and Sudan. After so much exposure to violence, he argued, it becomes ingrained in a child's mind. Violence becomes a survival mechanism: kill or be killed.

Another witness had produced a documentary titled "Ghetto 101" about growing up in the South Side. It played to a nationwide audience on National Public Radio. He told us that he was one of the few lucky young men who managed to escape the South Side without

committing any violent crimes. Yet another witness, a community or-
ganizer who had worked alongside Barack Obama when he was a
rookie politician in Chicago, told us that all the amenities of our suburban enclave didn't exist in the South Side. No safe parks, no recre-
ational activities, and not even any grocery stores.

Teachers from Robert's schools testified as did little league coaches and clergy from neighborhood churches. Then there was a raft, a
drifting mass, of childhood friends, uncles, cousins, and even Robert's
grandmother, who was too frail to travel, so she testified by video. All
of them said the same thing: to grow up in the South Side of Chicago
meant living constantly on the edge of disaster and death. This life
meant that young men like Robert grew up simply accustomed to evil
and violence.

I cannot overstate how often this message was given to us during
the two-week period of defense mitigation. Repetition can be powerful, but also numbing. Nearly all of the defense witnesses would start
out with what we in the jury eventually called "the South Side speech"
or "the Circle speech." Witnesses would introduce themselves and then
the defense attorney would place a large map of Chicago on an easel.
This was our signal that we were about to get the speech. Sometimes
the speech would last only a few minutes. Sometimes it went on for
an hour or more. More than a few times, I would see other jurors roll
their eyes as the map came out. Not again. Not the South Side speech.

I suppose it is true, then, that familiarity breeds contempt. When
the trial began many weeks before, everything was new, and I was
in awe of all the proceedings. Every word from an attorney seemed
noteworthy, and my hand ached with all the notes I was taking. After
a few weeks, though, routine set in. At this point, the difference between real courtrooms and Hollywood ones set in—most noticeably,
how much slower real life was than television. Around weeks six and
seven, I began to think that the attorneys on both sides were doing
things specifically to annoy me. I knew this couldn't possibly be true,

as this would of course be counter-productive for any attorney. But I had to wonder when the same questions were asked over and over, and the map of Chicago was dragged out for the umpteenth time.

During one long, hot afternoon session, I finally could not contain my frustration. As the Chicago map was placed on the easel yet again, and another witness restarted the catalog of horrors that is the South Side, I wrote in my notebook, "Another damn, fucking rehash of gangs and violence in Chicago." I then drew a crude depiction of a giant vortex, with little stick figure people being sucked into it. Below the vortex I wrote in ominous dark lettering, "BEWARE THE CIRCLE!" I didn't realize that an alternate juror sitting next to me was looking down at my notebook as I drew. She stifled a laugh but then looked at me with a shocked expression. Yes, I had written the word "fucking." It was the first time I can remember any of us on the jury using a curse word in any way.

Despite my fatigue with the repetition, I fully understood that life could be rough in Chicago. But I had a hard time imagining what it was like growing up there until I heard from Kendrick, one of Robert's two older brothers. Kendrick was out on parole after serving time for various drug charges (he has since completed his sentence). Although a big man, he was soft-spoken. He told us that his time in jail had given him a new perspective, and he was determined to turn his life around. He had regrets for the way he had lived, and for lost opportunities, including the chance he squandered to play college football.

Kendrick was the first defense witness I heard who said anything like this, who didn't immediately blame drugs, gangs, or the Windy City itself. Instead, he told stories about his little brother Robert, including what his family referred to as "the 31st Street incident."

Even in the midst of all the South Side violence, young Robert Ray still wanted to be a kid. Like me, he wanted to try his hand at fishing. One day when he was ten, Robert found a fishing rod, some tackle, and a bait bucket in a storage closet of one of the apartments. He knew that there was a big lake near where he lived. It was Lake Michigan, of course. There must be fish in that lake, he reasoned. Robert had heard people mention the 31st Street beach before, but he didn't know it would be a major effort to get there. The journey involved crossing many busy streets, going through a tunnel underneath a major highway, and of course, traversing the territory of a few gangs. He figured with childlike simplicity that all he needed to do was find 31st Street and head downhill toward the lake.

A family friend happened to spot Robert as he walked down 31st Street. It was such an incongruous sight, the friend had to laugh. There on a chaotic, dirty Chicago street was a young boy strutting along as if he was on a country lane, fishing pole slung over his shoulder and bait bucket swinging by his side, catching glints of sunlight. Robert's mother was soon on the scene, giving him a harsh scolding for taking such a dangerous trek on his own.

Kendrick laughed softly as he told us this story. "He had never been fishing before and didn't even know what to do with a fishing pole or a hook," Kendrick said with a smile. "He didn't even have any bait. I guess he thought he'd figure it all out when he got to the beach." This was Robert's character, Kendrick explained. Robert was inquisitive, smart, and fearless. He was the kind of person who would find a fishing pole, and even though he lived in a concrete jungle, would say to himself, "Fishing sounds fun. Why not?"

I looked at Robert while his brother talked about the 31st Street incident. Robert had a broad smile on his face, and he regarded his brother with a satisfied look. There was a flicker of life in his eyes. He covered his mouth with his hand, suddenly conscious that he was smiling.

This was the first time I had ever seen any expression from Robert Ray. Until that moment, he sat through weeks of testimony with no sign that he heard any of it. Nothing seemed to move him. Not the witnesses who, with trembling voices, described the painful, bloody death of Javad and Vivian. Not the autopsy photos. Not the grim-faced detectives who showed us ammunition cartridges and what they found in Robert's car. Not the grieving mothers of the victims who wept on the witness stand. He sat before us a convicted murderer, his attorneys striving to convince us to spare his life, and yet he appeared stone-faced through all of it. But at that moment, his face beamed with emotion—happiness. It was as though he and his brother were sitting around the dinner table with the family. They were sharing stories about Robert and his mischievous childhood adventures, laughing loudly and pushing their chairs back from the table, having eaten their fill.

The realization of what I had just seen hit me hard, even though it should have been obvious. Robert was someone's brother. He was once a child, innocent and carefree. Somewhere in my consciousness, I knew he was all these things before, but now I *saw* it as he smiled at his brother. A flicker of life and relationship.

The moment caused me to remember something I had once learned about Christ, someone I had given little thought to for many years. The Bible says that when Christ looked at people, he saw beyond their sins and problems to their innate humanity, a person created in God's very image. He was not deterred in ministering to anyone, even if they were lepers.

Again, my experience in the jury box prompted me to look beyond my past and the strict rules-and-regulations of the fundamentalist brand of Christianity to see compassion, mercy, humanity. But here I was in a courtroom, a place of judgment, where I would be asked to deliver justice. Justice was potentially at odds with compassion. A quiet dread settled over me as I sat in front of a crowded courtroom and wondered how it is possible to perform such a balancing act. To be just yet compassionate. To punish crime yet be *humane*.

During Kendrick's testimony, Robert's lead attorney would turn toward the jury, a mournful hound-dog look in his eyes. He would let out a small sigh and nod his head gently as if to say, "See, my client is not a monster. He just wanted a normal childhood like yours. He just wanted someone to take him fishing."

At least this is what I imagined he was trying to say. I don't know how the lawyer knew to emphasize the fishing story; I didn't write anything on my jury questionnaire about growing up in the country, living near a river, or fishing. A question was nagging me: what if someone had taken Robert fishing when he was a boy? It seemed quite a stretch to think that a fishing trip could save a boy from a life of gangs and drugs in one of the most violent places in America. But what if it could? What if a simple fishing trip showed Robert there was a world outside the concrete jungle? Could that have deflected him, if ever so slightly, from a life dedicated to crime?

I could scarcely fathom the depravity required to commit multiple murders. Perhaps I could not imagine it because violence had never entered my life. I could run around in the country as a boy and throw a fishing line into a river without worry of gangs or gunshots. The experts would probably tell me that violence was so foreign to me because, well, I grew up in a nonviolent place.

What if I had grown up in Chicago, and Robert had grown up in the countryside of Northern Colorado? Would he be the saint and I the sinner? Could a mere accident of birth be the only thing that set us apart?

As the defense team concluded their first week of mitigation testimony, I began to recognize a change in me, one that had long been forming. I knew that if Robert had appeared before my younger, more judgmental self, that there would have been no mitigation I would have accepted.

Coming out of my high-school and college years, I couldn't understand how anyone could sin. Take, for example, premarital sex, which my conservative, fundamentalist church taught was clearly sin. Wasn't it just a simple choice, then, to keep myself out of situations where that might be tempting? Yes, it made dating quite difficult, but as the Bible said, "All discipline for the moment seems not to be joyful, but sorrowful; yet to those who have been trained by it, afterwards it yields the peaceful fruit of righteousness" (Hebrews 12:11). Behavior was a matter of simple choice. I could choose the fruit of righteousness. With such a black-and-white view of the world, there was no mitigation for sin, especially not murder.

But these ideas about choices, discipline, and mitigation came before I had experienced my own failings in life. Until then my judgmental outlook on life was based on a mere theoretical understanding of sin and judgment. I never before had to decide on an actual punishment for any sinner. I never once had to levy a fine. Or impose a detention. Or expel someone from a group. During that trial, I had the power to send a sinner to his death, and that new power was terrifying and paralyzing. As a young man, I confidently railed against sin, preaching actual sermons in my conservative Christian school and church. That young man would have coolly quoted "the wages of sin is death" (Romans 6:23).

That young man was gone. In his place was a grown-up and broken man who wondered how it was possible to balance justice with mercy, and how a punishment as severe as death could ever be handed down by a mere mortal.

With these thoughts in my mind, it seemed more than coincidence that the last witness called by the defense was a pastor named Bruce Fulman. Reverend Fulman had visited Robert in jail many times. When he took the witness stand, Robert smiled back, providing the second and last time I would see any facial expressions from Robert Ray during the entire ten-week ordeal. Rev. Fulman told us of his meetings with Robert and how he believed Robert was improving as a person, even from jail. This wasn't the first time we had heard testimony like this. The defense had also called several prison officials who testified that Robert was a cooperative, model prisoner who took anger management classes for which he earned top grades. He read voraciously and took every class available to him. The lead defense attorney asked his final question of the trial to Reverend Fulman.

"Are any of us in a position to judge?"

"No, because it is all too complicated, the Reverend replied. "We would need God's knowledge in order to judge."

twelve
Victim Impact

"Your honor, the people call Christine Myong Wolfe." Christine, the mother of Vivian, stepped gingerly up to the witness box in front of me, threading her way around the chairs and desks in the front of the courtroom. Without any prompting, she stood before the judge and raised her right hand. She had clearly done this before. She waited there with her hand raised, just a few feet in front of the man who was found guilty of murdering her daughter. Her hand and forearm were wrapped in a tan bandage and splint, like the kind used to help people with chronic wrist pain.

The judge stood and took a step to the side of his large chair and spoke quickly and plainly. "Do you solemnly swear or affirm that the testimony you are about to give is the truth, the whole truth, and nothing but the truth? If so, say I do."

"I do." Her voice was faint, but I detected an Asian accent. She wore a soft white blouse beneath a dark blue jacket. Her dark hair was cut short and neatly styled, framing a face that was smooth of wrinkles yet heavy with weariness.

Christine's appearance occurred on what would be the last day of testimony in the trial which had begun nearly two months before. She was one of many witnesses who came to tell us about victim impact—how their lives had been changed after the murders of Javad and Vivian. We already heard from Javad's family, and now it was time to hear from Vivian's.

John Hower, the prosecutor, began by placing a large framed photograph of Vivian on an easel. It was her high school senior portrait. Vivian looked out at me from her perch on the easel with a shy smile and dark, sparkling eyes, her black hair pulled back into a bun. She wore a dark purple dress, and a thin, gold braided necklace. Vivian was the perfect blending of her Korean mother and African-American father. She had soft, light brown skin and an Asian nose and eyes.

"Your honor, I object," came a voice from the defense table. "The picture is prejudicial."

An exasperated sigh arose from the prosecution's table. I was also caught by surprise. How could anyone object to this? To Vivian? The judge rarely discussed objections within earshot of the jury. He called the lawyers over to the bench, and they whispered their arguments back and forth while we waited. We had endured this countless times in the preceding two months.

As the lawyers argued *sotto voce*, I watched Christine. She rolled her eyes and shook her head in disgust at the objection. Then her face settled on an expressionless state as she waited, with her hands folded in her lap, and her posture relaxed. She had testified before in front of Sir Mario Owens, Robert Ray's accomplice and hit man, and seemed unsurprised by the antics from the lawyers. The judge soon overruled the objection with no explanation, so I never understood why the defense considered Vivian's picture to be prejudicial.

Prosecutor Hower asked for a few biographical details about Vivian before asking, "What were some of her favorite activities?"

"She loved to be outside, to hike and go camping." Christine's expressionless state now brightened a bit.

Hower put up another picture of Vivian. This time she was dressed in swim gear and standing near a yellow and blue raft that was beached on the edge of a river.

"Objection, your honor. Prejudicial." The defense attorney said this sheepishly, pushing himself up halfway to standing with both hands on the desk.

"Noted, but overruled." The judge responded without pause or even a glance toward the attorney.

Christine continued, unperturbed. "Ah yes, I remember this was after we had gone rafting the summer before she was…" Her voice trailed off for a moment. "The summer before she was murdered. I know this picture was taken *after* we went rafting because of the beer." I smiled a bit, noticing that Vivian held a can of beer in her hand, barely visible in the corner of the photo. "She loved Colorado and the mountains. And she was always wanting to go outside. I couldn't get her to stay inside even when the weather was bad."

"Do you do outdoor activities anymore? Hiking?"

"No." Christine looked down. "Hiking and camping were what we did together. Now what's the point?"

John Hower placed another poster-sized picture of Vivian on the easel, in place of the rafting picture. This time Vivian cuddled a small dog, their faces meshed together, Vivian's hair spilling over the dog's back. The dog wore a pink sweater.

"Objection…"

"Overruled."

"Is this Vivian's dog in the picture with her?" Hower asked.

"Yes, this is Coco. She loved Coco."

"Can you tell us how Coco came into her life?"

Christine straightened in her chair. "When Vivian went to college at Colorado State University, I gave her a credit card to be used strictly for emergencies only." Christine emphasized the words again for impact, "Emergency. Only."

"One day I was looking at the credit card statement, and I saw a charge from a pet store. How could this be an emergency? Do you know what she had done?" Christine gestured toward the picture. "She bought this Chihuahua dog! And she bought clothes for it, too. I never thought there could be such fancy clothes for a dog. I asked her why she used the emergency-only credit card, and do you know what she said to me?"

She paused on this question, her face brightening a bit in anticipation, as though about to tell us the punchline to a joke. "My daughter told me very seriously, 'Mom, I needed this dog. It was an emergency.'"

Christine flashed a grin and looked over at the gallery to her friends and family. She laughed softly for a moment as many in the gallery laughed along with her. I leaned back in my chair and smiled back at the picture of Vivian and her fashionable pup.

Christine continued when the laughter subsided. "That is…*was*… Vivian's personality. If she could do something to make her life better or someone else's life better, she just did it. She just wanted everyone to be happy. She loved everything and everyone that could be loved."

"Where is this dog now?" Hower asked.

"Of course, we still have it." Her smile by now had disappeared. "I am reminded every day of Vivian when the dog comes up to me, wagging her tail." Her voice was strained, and her eyes dampened with tears. She paused to steady herself. "And…and…I'm terrified that this dog will die someday. It is all I have of her. My daughter. What will I have left when the dog is gone?" She cried quietly behind the picture of Vivian and Coco the emergency Chihuahua.

When she was dismissed from the stand, the defense declining to cross-examine her, she shuffled back to her seat. There was no sign of relief on her tear-streaked face.

Christine's testimony was just one of many tearful recollections of Javad and Vivian we heard from their mothers, fathers, siblings, extended family, and friends. The last witness was Mike Prosser, Vivian's stepfather. Vivian's father died when she was only two months old, and when Christine remarried a few years later, Mike became the only father she had ever known.

Mike's testimony was the opposite of Christine's—forceful and fiery. "The emotional pain of losing a child was just the beginning," he told us. "I didn't have a clue what it was like to lose a child until I stood in the hospital and watched them take her body to the coroner's office." As he spoke, his voice grew in volume until it filled the room. With his white hair and beard and impassioned delivery, he reminded me of a street preacher or end-time prophet. He spoke for ten minutes precisely cataloging the specific impact the court cases had on their lives. The constant subpoenas to testify. The endless days in the courtroom. Reliving the details of Vivian's death over and over.

"I am not merely frustrated," he said leaning forward and nearly standing, "I am furious." The defense attorneys again declined to cross-examine.

♦ ♦ ♦

In the United States, a convicted criminal has the right to *allocution*— to speak directly to the people about to decide his punishment. The morning after the families had given their victim impact testimonies, Robert stood to address us. He rose awkwardly, hobbled apparently by lower back pain. I didn't know at the time that his legs were chained to the floor. After he stood, he quietly looked toward the judge waiting for a signal to begin. His lawyer stood to his left and placed his hand on Robert's shoulder. I closed my notebook and set it on my lap.

I wanted to give him my full attention and listen undistracted by note taking. Robert stood about six feet tall and his thin frame disappeared inside clothes that seemed a size too large: khaki pants and a white, button-down shirt loosely tucked-in. At long last, we heard the voice of the man at the center of everything the last two months.

His voice surprised me—a soft tenor, quiet and slow. We could barely hear him. I was expecting more force, more power from this man who commanded a drug dealing business and had a hand in three murders, beginning with the death of Greg Vann at Lowry Park.

"I want to say something to the moms," he said.

He looked over his right shoulder at the front row where Rhonda Fields and Christine Wolfe normally sat. But they were not there. There were no other family members present either, the first time in the entire trial this had happened. I realized this was probably on purpose. They didn't want to hear from Robert. As if to emphasize the boycott of the allocution, all but one of the prosecutors were also absent.

Only the lead prosecutor remained at the desk, and he typed on his laptop, looking down at the screen through the bottom of his bifocal glasses. The typing was a steady, pounding rhythm interrupted every few seconds by jabs at the backspace key. I couldn't imagine what required so much typing, right here in the court at this dramatic moment. Was he doing this on purpose?

Robert turned back to his lawyer, dismayed. "Where are the moms?" he said in an intense whisper. Perhaps he wasn't aware we could still hear him, if only just barely.

The lawyer shrugged. "They're not here," he whispered back.

"Well then why the fuck am I even standing here?"

There was a pause. The lawyer had a grim expression on his face. For a moment, I was shocked, thinking to myself, "Well, Mr. Ray, because you are the fuck on trial for your life. That's why." As soon as the thought flashed through my mind, I also realized he didn't care about me. He only seemed concerned about the moms.

"What do I do?" Robert asked his attorney. "Do I keep going anyway?" The attorney whispered something to Robert, who cocked his head to the side to hear it. After about twenty seconds, Robert continued his speech. He looked over the top of the judge at the back wall of the courtroom, his eyes shifting back and forth but never looking toward me, the rest of the jury, or anyone else.

"I'm sorry this happened, especially about the girl." I assumed he meant Vivian, although he didn't say her name. "We didn't know about her or who she was." These words came out of Robert quickly, as though he needed to say them before he lost his nerve. I wondered, was he confessing somehow?

"I guess I'd say just go ahead and stick the needle in me." Despite the seriousness of what he was saying, the words came out of Robert soft and flat. "The prison is inhumane. It is a warehouse where they put people in little cages. They treat us like animals. I don't know why I'd want to grow old there. But then I think that maybe I could still do some good. Maybe I could still talk to people before it is too late for them. Maybe I could help people stay away from what happened to me. So…I guess I'm sayin' I still want to live."

The lawyer gazed at Robert, nodded his head gently, and patted him on the shoulder. Robert said, "That's all I have to say," and sat back down quickly but silently, his hands clasped together tightly in his lap.

I wanted a sign that Robert connected with the pain or grief that the death of Javad and Vivian caused. Or that he would even say their names. Or that he would acknowledge his role in the whole tragic mess. No such acknowledgment would ever come. I wanted more from him. More connection, more emotion, more *anything.*

I knew he was capable of communicating powerfully. During the trial, several poems and rap songs Robert had written in jail were entered into evidence. They were angry and full of rage about the unfairness of life and the harsh consequences for petty crimes. He was punished once in prison because he had somehow gotten possession of a marker and wrote "Fuck Arapahoe County" on his cell walls. He had a voice apparently some time ago, but it was gone the moment he stood before me with a chance to influence how I thought about him. I wanted him to try and give me a reason to spare his life. I wanted him to show me he cared, that this mattered to him. Even if he yelled and screamed. Even if he looked directly at me and snarled, "And in closing, fuck you, juror number twelve!"

Instead, he seemed to be daring me to do *whatever the fuck* I wanted. He seemed to be floating above it all. Above the one hundred and eleven witnesses. Above the thousands of pages of evidence, hundreds of photographs, and dozens of physical artifacts. Above the jury. Above me. "Do your job," he seemed to be saying to me. "Whatever."

This aloofness and ambivalence angered and saddened me all at once. It wasn't *whatever* to me. I didn't want this job of judgment. If I decided to kill him, I would be the one who would have to think about it long after Robert was dead, wondering if I had made the right choice. All I could do now was try to parse his uncertain words. *I guess I'm sayin' I still want to live.* This is a guess? You don't know if you want to live? *Help people stay away from what happened to me.* This crime, two murders and the one before—they just *happened* to you? You didn't have any role in plotting for nearly a year the intimidation and killing of a witness against you? You didn't get your best friend and entire family involved in a crime that would only benefit you? You are a victim in all this?

Robert's speech raised more questions than answers. Ultimately, I thought he did want to live, and his shaky performance was due to the nerves and pressure of this high stakes situation.

His lawyers seemed to care, and they were absolutely certain what their client wanted. They argued passionately for us to spare his life.

"Is it really moral for us to take someone's life when they no longer pose a threat?" the lead defense attorney asked us during his closing arguments. "Life in prison without parole is a very harsh sentence. Another killing is not going to do any good. Please, no more killing. No more death."

◆　◆　◆

Before we started our final deliberations, we had a day when we were dismissed a few hours early so the judge and attorneys could finalize the jury instructions. I could have used the time to go home and take a nap, but instead I decided to go to my office.

I had not talked to anyone at work for over a month now. My job at a large software company, the one that was still paying my salary while I was on jury duty, seemed like another lifetime ago.

I did stay more connected during the first month of the trial. I tried to keep tabs on what was happening with my team as they worked on a new software product we were preparing for launch. In the first few weeks of the trial, I checked my email and returned phone calls during breaks and lunch. When I arrived home during that first month, I started my laptop and worked on software specifications or answering customer questions. As the weeks wore on, though, I stopped checking-in because I was overwhelmed by the daily deluge of evidence, witnesses, and arguments. I had no mental strength left to deal with anything and certainly not another job.

I walked into the office building, marveling at the opulence compared to the beat-up courthouse. I was stunned by the polished marble floors, high ceilings, and light pouring in from tall windows. It also seemed strange to me to enter a building and not have to pass through security screening. There was no deputy to escort me. Nobody set down their things and rose to their feet when I entered the room. I snuck into the office through a side door and slipped into the chair at my desk. Nothing had changed since I was last there two months ago. I donned my phone headset and dialed-in to my team's weekly conference call a few minutes late. We met by phone since the team was scattered across North America.

As with most conference call systems, a chime announced that someone had connected to the call.

"Who just joined the call?" I recognized the voice of my boss.

"Hi everyone. It's Carl." There was a chorus of *heys* and *hellos*.

"This is great, Carl, are you finally back?"

"We have a break this afternoon, and then I'm back to court tomorrow." Anticipating the next several questions, I added, "And I think I'll be out at least another few days. Unfortunately, I can't tell you anything else."

"We'll take what we can get. We are just glad to have you here for now."

The team continued with their call as I listened. The topic was something about passwords and password policies. Should we make users change their passwords? How often? I looked out the window at the I-25 highway fourteen floors below me. The highway began to fill with late afternoon traffic.

I stared out the window, my eyes fixed on nothing in particular. I thought about Sylvia Marshall, Javad's grandmother. She needed help getting into the witness chair as she dragged a canister of oxygen behind her. She walked hunched over and moved slowly and painfully. But she was impeccably dressed, jewelry glistening. I could imagine this is how she would look for church.

"How did you hear of your grandson's murder?" the prosecutor asked her.

Sylvia looked at him with a patient but sad expression. "I wish I could tell you."

"You don't remember?"

"I don't remember a single thing about that night. I'm afraid I must have blocked it all from my memory."

Sylvia paused for a second and caught her breath, exhaling through her mouth and inhaling through her nose. She adjusted the oxygen tube that ran over her ears to her nostrils. "They said I acted terrible that night." Sylvia glanced toward her family in the gallery. Her voice cracked. "They said I was yellin' and screamin' and carryin' on. I suppose I was."

"Maybe we should take a moment to get Carl caught up on the password issue." I was jolted back to the conference call by my boss. I tried to concentrate. Apparently, the password discussion was still going on. As I listened, I imagined that the discussion was taking place in court with attorneys arguing strenuously.

"Ladies and gentlemen of the jury, if we require users to change passwords every ninety days, our help desk will be overwhelmed with support calls."

"Objection, your honor. That is speculation."

My concentration waned again, and I leaned back in my chair and stared out the window once more, the cord to my headset stretched out as far as it could go. I could see my reflection in the glass. I stared at myself for a moment. My thoughts didn't wander. Instead, they appeared in my mind like a parade of pictures on a screen, much like the vision I had before the trial: Javad's "Sacrifice" tattoo. Vivian's hair in a ponytail as her head rested on a blue foam block on the stainless-steel autopsy table. Sheri Majors shaking in fear as she testified before Robert Ray. A black and yellow Pittsburgh Steelers football jersey. One of Javad's friends had torn it off his body and thrown it to the ground in anger and grief when he came running up to the crime scene and saw Javad's car streaked with blood. Robert Ray's wife as she suddenly ran from the witness stand, unable to control her sobbing. The lawyer's hand on Robert's shoulder as Robert tried to speak in front of us. The images would not relent.

"Carl, you have a lot of experience with our customers. What would they think of our options here?" Again, the voice of my boss.

I broke eye contact with my reflection in the window and faced the phone, staying silent. My finger hovered above the disconnect button.

"Carl?"

My throat tightened, and nervous energy shot through my chest. I hit the button and hung up on the call. Then I yanked the headset off and flung it to the back of my desk. I pulled the palms of my hands down my forehead and over my eyes to my chin. *I can't believe I'm here talking about fucking passwords.*

Until that moment, my career was the major focus of my life. I worked hard to build a reputation and maximize my earnings, which I had done remarkably well. In that moment, my career felt petty and small compared to the devastation and impact of murder. My life's work felt empty, and I realized I didn't care about it anymore.

I hated my old job at the software company. I hated my new job at the courthouse. I hated everything, and I felt damned. I was damned if I chose the death penalty because that would offend about half of the people with a stake in the case. I was damned if I chose life in prison because the other half would be angry with me. Why the hell would I care about passwords or anything related to building a software product?

When most people have a bad day at work, they can let off steam over a beer with colleagues or vent to their spouse—but not me. The judge prohibited us from discussing anything about the case with anyone. I hadn't said a word about it for months. I didn't even tell anyone what trial I was on. "It's a criminal case," is all I said to anyone who asked.

What a terrifically cruel thing to do, I thought to myself. Forcibly conscript people to a job, bombard them daily with tales of death and grief for week after week, give them an impossible choice, and then tell them to bottle up all their feelings.

Many times, in my relationship with Molly, she would say that I didn't need anyone. Sometimes she said this with tears and frustration, other times with a sober matter-of-factness. Sometimes she would wonder aloud if I had any feelings at all. Now I wanted desperately to talk about what I was feeling. I decided that I was tired of acting like the ideal Christian. Tired of pretending I didn't have any failures. Tired of protecting my righteous reputation.

I sat at my desk surrounded by people and activity but felt completely isolated and alone.

thirteen
AGGRAVATING FACTORS

G etting to death row is not easy. To land a spot there, a jury must vote unanimously on three different decisions.

The prerequisite, of course, is that a person must be convicted of first-degree murder after deliberation. The "after deliberation" part refers not to the jury's deliberation, but to the defendant's. In other words, the defendant killed another person intentionally after reflection and judgment on the act. They thought about the murder and proceeded anyway. They had time to change course. Obviously, we had already voted unanimously that Robert Ray was guilty of two counts, one for the murder of Javad, one for Vivian. That meant we had another trial and three decisions to make.

First, the jury must agree that there is at least one "aggravating factor" in the murder that made it especially grievous and worthy of the harshest punishment. There are seventeen possible aggravating factors in Colorado law. These include the use of an unlawful weapon, lying in wait, trying to conceal a crime, or knowingly endangering others. After only an hour of deliberation, we decided unanimously that there were aggravating factors in each of the two murders.

Second, the jury must decide if the mitigating factors outweigh the aggravating factors. The defense team spent two weeks building the mitigation case: growing up in the "war zone" of Chicago's South Side, brain injuries, and so on. A "yes" vote meant that a juror believed the mitigation case was strong enough to outweigh the aggravating factors. All it would take is one "yes" vote, and the death penalty would not be imposed. There would be one vote for each of the two murders.

Finally, provided we got this far, the third and final vote would be a simple one: should the defendant be sentenced to death or life in prison without the possibility of parole? If there were twelve votes for the death penalty, then it would be so. If even one juror voted for life in prison, then that is the punishment the defendant would receive. In this vote, unlike all the dozens of others we conducted in the previous deliberations, there were no legal standards. Each juror was to decide for herself or himself what was the right and moral choice. A juror could vote either way for no other reason than they just felt like it. Further, there was no duty on the part of the juror to explain or justify their decision.

The personal nature of this last decision made me nervous. I wondered what I would do if a single juror decided to vote differently than all the others and simply refuse to discuss it.

I would soon get a chance to find out.

◆　◆　◆

For Javad's case, we only needed an hour to determine the answer to the second question: do the mitigating factors outweigh the aggravating factors? We were unanimous that the answer was no. This meant we would, in Javad's case, proceed to the third decision, whether he should get the death penalty or life without parole.

For Vivian's case, I also argued that the answer to the second question was also no. According to Colorado law, one of the aggravating factors in a murder is extreme indifference and knowingly endangering others. I thought this was rather clear-cut.

In the thirty-six hours before Javad was murdered, Robert Ray and his gang became increasingly bold in confronting him. Robert asked his wife and a friend to track Javad down at a park in Aurora where he was at a Father's Day barbeque and auto show. Robert wanted them to stare Javad down, try to talk to him, and even offer him money on the spot to skip out on his testimony. They did this in broad daylight in a crowded public park. Next, they tried confronting him at Gibby's, a busy restaurant. Finally, they killed him as he was driving in a residential neighborhood at a time when most people were home.

They must have known that the hail of gunfire along a residential street would put a lot of others at risk. Despite this, they had chosen bold and open confrontations in public because they were desperate to stop Javad. Furthermore, they were extraordinarily lucky that the murder count was not four people instead of only two. Javad and Vivian were driving that night to meet a friend and her infant daughter for dinner. Javad offered to drive them all to the restaurant together, but the friend did not want the hassle of moving her daughter's car seat to Javad's car. If not for that decision, those dozen bullets would have entered a car occupied by one man, two women, and a baby.

Javad's murder would have been bad enough if they had killed him in some isolated field with nobody else around for miles. To blithely assume that nobody else was in the car and then spray the neighborhood with lead—well, that made it worse. Vivian died because of, as the law puts it, extreme indifference.

But Rick did not share my opinion. "I...I don't know, guys," he said. "I just don't see it this way."

Rick pushed his chair back from the table and leaned forward with his elbows on his knees. Rick was about ten years older than me, wore glasses, and kept his graying black hair neatly parted. Like me, he was in a computer software profession. I liked Rick. I had voted for him to be the foreperson because I thought he would be the most likely to think like I do.

"What makes Vivian's death any different than Javad's?" I asked.

"They didn't know about Vivian. There's no evidence they knew she was in the car. Yes, technically it was first-degree murder because Vivian died in the course of another first-degree murder, but I'm not sure they intended to kill her." Rick did not look up as he spoke. He stared at the middle of the table.

I straightened in my chair at the edge of my seat. "So, are you saying that Vivian's death wasn't as bad as Javad's?"

"That's not what I'm saying at all." Rick sat upright. "Her murder was just as bad. I'm only saying that it was *different.* I don't think I can vote with you on this one." Rick's gaze was still vaguely toward the center of the table, away from me.

I glanced around the room and noticed that nobody appeared to want to press this like I did. I wanted more of an explanation. I thought this would be unfair to Vivian. How could we say that her death was somehow less aggravated than Javad's? They were sitting together when they were shot, and they were killed for the same reason.

"I don't know, Rick, it sure sounds like you think Vivian's death wasn't as bad. Otherwise why would you disagree?"

"Look, don't put words into my mouth." Rick's eyes finally looked up to meet mine. "Vivian's death was tragic. We just disagree on this technical aspect. That's all."

"No, you look," I shot back, my voice tinged with anger and disbelief. "It's one thing if you don't want the death penalty for Vivian's murder. That is your right. But don't do that now. Let us at least get to the third vote so we can debate it. You can always vote no during the third and final vote."

Rick slumped forward again, his elbows on his knees.

"But what you are doing—you are single-handedly preventing us from even having the discussion about punishment for Vivian's murder," I said. "What are we going to tell Vivian's family? What am I going to tell Christine Wolfe, that Vivian's death was less aggravated than Javad's? That there was no extreme indifference to her life? How are we going to explain that we couldn't even take the final vote for her daughter?"

Rick popped out of his chair to his feet. "This conversation is over. I'm officially taking a break." Rick took a few quick steps into the bathroom and shut the door.

There was a reason why Rick said he was taking a break. The judge had told us that we could not deliberate unless everyone was present. If one person needed a break, we all had to take a break and stop talking about the case. This was Rick's way of ending the debate, with me being powerless to do anything about it.

I grew angry as I sat in front of ten other shocked and silent jurors. I could just picture Christine's face and hear her quiet voice. "How could you say my daughter's death was not aggravated? How could you all decide that the defendant had a better case than my daughter?"

I bit my lower lip and closed my eyes, trying to remain calm. I wanted to yell. Or cry. I didn't know how I would decide in the final vote—life or death—but I believed we owed Christine Wolfe at least the dignity of taking that final vote on her daughter's behalf.

After a few minutes, someone at the table finally broke the silence. "How long is he going to be in there?"

"I don't know. We might as well take an official break."

We stood up and started to move around. Greg wanted a smoke break. I called for the bailiff, so we could go to the patio. Like the judge said, we all had to stick together. When the bailiff arrived, Rick emerged from the bathroom, and we all walked down to the smoking area in single-file, saying nothing. We stood on the patio, penned in by a ten-foot high wall. Greg sucked on his cigarette quickly while the rest of us shuffled around the patio not speaking or even looking at each other.

I started to feel bad for snapping at Rick. I thought about the time during the jury selection process when I did my individual interviews with both sets of lawyers. One of the defense attorneys had made a point to grill me about bullying. "Are you going to bully another juror who wants to give my client mercy?" I remembered him startling me with his suddenly loud voice. "What if there is one person—*one person*—who doesn't agree with everyone else? You are going to pressure that person to change their decision, aren't you? *Aren't you?*"

Now the exact scenario the attorney had raised was actually happening. I was not going to prove him right. I was not going to be a bully. After all, it was I who instituted the "have courage" rule. I told the jury during our very first deliberations a month ago, "have courage, and say what you need to even if you are the only one." I realized I was not going to get my way, and I thought Rick was wrong, but I could not fault him for having the courage I had asked the jury to have.

My eyes became teary as I thought about Vivian. The same image seemed to come to my mind every time I thought of her. Lying on the steel table, her head propped up on a blue foam block, her hair still pulled into a ponytail. I tried instead to think of her by the side of the river, drinking a cold one after a day of rafting.

We all filed back into the jury room after about fifteen minutes and sat down. Everyone except Rick was looking at me. Lois had a look of disbelief on her face. Our eyes met across the table, and she shrugged and shook her head. Rick swiveled his chair around and was looking out the window, toward the football fields.

"Rick, is there anything else you want to say?" My voice was somber, barely loud enough to be heard across the room.

"Nope." Rick was motionless, staring out the window.

"Is there anything else you want to hear from us?"

"Nope." Again, motionless.

"So then are you completely decided that this is how you want to vote?"

"Yep."

I slumped back in my chair. "Well, then, we can stop talking about Vivian. We aren't going to make it past the second vote for her like we did for Javad."

The room remained quiet. Rick finally turned his chair around to face us. "It is official then," I said. I reached for the verdict form, and checked the box labeled "NOT UNANIMOUS" for vote #2—do the mitigating factors outweigh the aggravating factors? For the murder of Vivian Wolfe, the punishment would be life in prison without the possibility of parole. We would not take the third and final vote for Vivian. But we did have one vote left in Javad's case.

We needed another break, even though the last one was barely fifteen minutes ago. As the group stood up, a few people snapped their notebooks closed with a sharp slap. I heard a few heavy sighs. "Well, at least that part is over," someone said.

This time, as we marched downstairs, there was a bit of chatter between us. I was looking for some way to thaw my relationship with Rick. I was hoping that something would happen to re-energize the group. The last decision seemed to drain the energy from us.

We walked out onto the patio yet again. Greg lit up another cigarette. This time Vicki and Steven joined him. They had both quit smoking years before. The stress of the trial, though, had sent them right back for a nicotine fix to calm their nerves.

"Man, I feel terrible for getting you guys back into smoking." Greg handed a cigarette to Vicki.

"Don't feel bad, Greg. I need this." She leaned over so Greg could light it for her.

We could see a slice of the clear blue sky beyond the ten-foot brick wall that kept us penned in on the patio. It was a beautiful late spring day—warm, with a slight breeze. The thought of getting outside was very tempting.

Marie could hardly take it. When we were allowed outside for lunch, back in the early part of the trial, she would walk the nearby open space, looking for birds, and eagerly reporting back to us what she had seen. "There's a hawk's nest in that tree right over there!" she told us one day after lunch. We all crowded at the jury room window to get a look.

Marie looked at the bailiff with a mournful face. "Please, please, please let us go outside for just a few minutes. We need to walk around and get some air."

The bailiff smiled but shook his head. "I'm sorry, but I can't let you out."

"Oh, c'mon, Pleeeeease!" Marie looked at me and then back at the bailiff. "Carl has ordered that we all go outside for a walk, and he *is* the foreperson." A few people laughed. Marie poked me in the shoulder. I looked at her and she pointed with an urgent gesture towards the top of the wall.

"Oh yeah, it's true." I turned toward the bailiff. "The judge said we are in charge of the deliberations. You better let us out, or we might climb the walls. You can't stop us all with only one Taser."

The bailiff laughed. "Let me see what I can do." He disappeared and returned a minute later with another deputy. "C'mon, let's go for a walk!"

Marie nearly screamed her approval.

There was a small lawn between the courthouse and the jail. A few trees were planted there, still too young to provide much shade. A sidewalk connected the courthouse to the main entrance of the jail. We started our little march down the sidewalk, being watched closely by the deputies. We passed by a small, grassy knoll that rose gradually about ten feet up from the sidewalk before sloping down again toward the parking lot.

I saw a blur of motion from the corner of my eye. Someone darted away from the group and up onto the knoll. It was Tonya. "I'm freeeeee!" she yelled as she dashed up the hill. The deputies froze, unsure of what to do. Was this really some sort of escape attempt? Would they give chase and tackle her? Use their Tasers?

When Tonya reached the top of the knoll, she turned around, extended her arms like wings, and skipped down the knoll back toward us. "I'm free, I'm freeee!" she yelled. Marie bolted from the group next. "C'mon, everyone!" Seconds later, there was a line of twelve jurors, following Tonya up and down the knoll, arms extended. "I'm free, I'm free," we all yelled.

The deputies looked frightened. I thought they might call for backup. They were probably imagining the headlines: "Tonight at ten, the bizarre story of a runaway jury."

In that moment, I did feel free. As fresh air filled my lungs and my heart revved up a bit, I decided I should be free, too. My entire life had been lived in a metaphorical courtroom where I judged other people according to religious law. As the ideal Christian boy, I grew up not understanding how people could make the decisions they did. They decided to have sex outside marriage. They decided to believe in evolution. They decided to do a hundred other things I thought were wrong at the time. I never had mercy for those people who disagreed with me. Instead of seeing the world from another person's perspective, I amped up the rhetoric and the preaching, redoubling my effort to convince them. Now my life was locked in a courtroom where a decision was just made that I did not agree with. I decided I would have mercy and accept Rick's decision. I felt free. I decided I had made a mistake devoting my life to arguing about religious law. I felt free.

To the bailiff's relief, we all descended the hill to the sidewalk after a minute. I was breathing heavily. Marie flopped on the ground and laid back, catching her breath. Soon we were all sitting or lying in the grass, looking up into the cloudless sky.

"I think we needed that," someone said.

"Yeah, thanks Tonya for the exercise," someone added.

Tonya laughed as she stood up. "Hey, I was actually trying to escape until I got to the top of the hill and realized how out of shape I am."

We headed back upstairs, this time making small talk like we always did. I walked over to Rick. "I hope we can start fresh. I hope there are no hard feelings and that you realize I respect you."

"I'm okay," he said. "And don't worry about it. This isn't easy for any of us."

We walked past the room where the alternate jurors were sitting, reading books or watching movies, trying to pass the time while we deliberated. They probably heard us coming from far away. Some of us were still catching our breath, while others were straightening clothes and smoothing hair. The alternates looked at us confused, and then at each other as if to say, "What is up with them?"

Each of us had arrived on this jury initially through random chance, our names being pulled from the list of registered voters in the county. They were strangers to me then, but I had grown very close to these eleven people. I was proud of how we were conducting ourselves. We were holding together under high stress. We could bounce back from a fight, and each of us was stepping up to help the group when we needed it. Once it was Vicki's thorough note-taking that helped us stay organized. Another time, Greg's quiet and concise observations got people to think. And now Tonya's spontaneous calisthenics had injected some life into our tired bodies and minds.

I liked these people. I felt protective of them and I wanted to keep us unified. I wanted us to respect each other. We were learning to depend on each other, and soon we would need that more than ever. We were about to discuss our final vote.

fourteen

LIFE OR DEATH

I drove to the courthouse on Friday June 5, squinting to see the eastbound traffic ahead of me in the bright morning sunshine.

"Just a half day today," I reminded the bailiff as he met me at the door.

Kelly had a job interview that afternoon and needed to be out of court at noon. Earlier in the trial, with everything new and uncertain, I would have *requested* the court to allow us out at noon. But now, as an experienced veteran juror, I *told* the court we would be dismissing at noon. *We're in charge now*, was my reasoning. Plus, I felt protective of the jury. We had already sacrificed so much in the previous ten weeks, I wasn't going to let this temporary job get in the way of Kelly's career.

Kelly's interview made me nervous for her. I already had my own breakdown at work, after the victim impact testimony. The stupid conference call about stupid password policies tipped me into a depression.

My job now felt pointless and petty compared to my trial experience. I knew I was going to have a hard time finding motivation for it again. How would it go now in a job interview?

I thought about a question I had once in an interview. As I sat in the jury room waiting for everyone to arrive, I imagined the same interview question posed to Kelly:

"Kelly, have you ever had to make a really tough decision at work? If so, how did you handle it?"

I imagined Kelly's answer: "I had to decide whether a convicted murder should live or die. How's that—enough of a tough decision for you?"

"Wow. Okay. Um, well, how did you handle that?" The interviewer shifted back in his chair, his hands on the edge of his desk, as if to put some distance between him and Kelly.

Kelly leaned forward, upright, narrowing the distance between them, her eyes wide. "How do you imagine I would handle it? I mean, think about it. You've got a man's life in your hands. What would you do? You can't possibly imagine the nuance, the variables, the expectations, and the total finality of the decision."

"Uh huh." The interviewer curled Kelly's resume into a tight scroll in his hands.

"It was agony, and I didn't *handle* it. I had no idea how to handle it. I cried all the time and wished to God that I didn't have to make the decision. I'm not even sure I made a decision as much as just realized over time what I was supposed to do."

The interviewer shrugged slightly, making his profile in the chair smaller. He let go of Kelly's resume, and it uncurled, opening on the desk. "Okay. And what did you eventually…"

"Does it matter?" Kelly cut him off, her voice rising. "If I tell you, there's a fifty-fifty chance you won't agree with me. You might even hate me for what I decided. Or maybe you'll think I'm a hero. How would you like it if every decision you made had these consequences—hate or hero? Have I ever made a tough decision? Ha! I should be asking you that question." Kelly's hair flew off her shoulders and framed her face as she shook her head. "And the answer would be no. No, you really haven't had to make a tough decision. You have no idea."

"Okay, then." The interviewer stood halfway up from his chair, making a slight gesture toward the door. "This has been a, uh, very interesting conversation, and, uh, we'll give you a call if we decide to move ahead with your application."

The imaginary scene in my mind was interrupted by a few other jurors entering the room. Now I wasn't sure if I was nervous for Kelly or nervous for me. The truth was that I didn't know what I was going to decide. I knew we would not vote today; we just didn't have time. We needed at least three hours after we voted to let the parties in the case arrive back at the court, have the verdicts read, and then wait for the traffic to clear before we would be set free. This would mean a vote would have to be taken by nine in order to be done by noon— Kelly's departure time for her interview. We hadn't even started the final deliberations yet, so this was simply not possible.

I felt relief, actually, that this day would not be the final day. I wanted more time to realize the decision. I wanted the thick fog to dissolve gradually with the morning sun, revealing the path ahead.

◆　◆　◆

"I'm not exactly sure how this day—our deliberations—will go," I said once we were all present around the table. "There's just one question left: do you want Robert Ray to get the death penalty for the murder of Javad Fields or not?"

Everyone stayed very still, as if even a tiny motion would signal a willingness to speak first.

"It's not a big deal." I joked trying to break the ice. "Just a simple yes or no question."

"Yeah right, reeeeeal simple." Big Dan laughed as he nudged my arm gently with his left elbow. "I don't know what I was so worried for!"

Now the room was alive again, with the jurors laughing just a bit, swiveling in their chairs, reaching for coffee mugs.

"I'll go first." Kelly stood up.

Thank God for that, I thought. I did not want to speak yet; the fog had not lifted for me. It hadn't for Kelly either.

Kelly reached across the table, straining for one of the evidence boxes. James gave the box a push toward her. We watched as she rummaged around, pulling out a few folders. She took two photographs and put them on the easel at the front of the room, right next to her chair. Both pictures were of Robert Ray. Kelly cleared her throat and faced the easel, still standing. "These are the two faces of Robert Ray," she said.

I recognized the first picture right away. It was the mug shot of Robert right after his arrest. He glared menacingly at the camera, his lips pressed tight and his eyes narrowed. We had seen this picture dozens of times. It was the default picture of him the prosecution always used. The second picture showed Robert at home, just a year or so before all the crime and mayhem. He was holding his toddler-age nephew to his side with one arm. The boy had his arms around Robert's neck and pressed his cheek to Robert's face with a delighted smile. Robert himself was smiling, and with his free hand he pointed at the camera playfully.

Kelly paused for a moment, and we stared at the pictures. "I don't know what to do," she said. She tapped the mug shot. "On one hand, Robert is a murderer." Kelly had turned to the side. I could not see her entire face, but I could see a small rivulet of tears running down her cheek. She smoothed the tears away with the tips of her fingers.

"He killed two people and he…" Kelly paused again, the tears pouring down uncontrollably, running to her neck. She dropped to her seat, facing the rest of us. She raised a shaking hand over her mouth for a moment before dropping it to her lap. "He did something incredibly evil, and there's just no excuse for it." Her voice was strained but loud. "On the other hand, I see what he was like before all this, before he became a murderer. He wasn't always like this, and I wonder if any of that Robert Ray is left."

Kelly paused again to wipe the tears from her face. Marie reached for a box of tissues that was sitting on the windowsill and placed it in front of Kelly. Marie took a few tissues herself and dabbed at the tears on her own face. "These are the same person." Kelly looked back at the two pictures of Robert Ray. "If all I knew was the murderer, I'd say sure, put him to death. But when I know something about him, I also want to have mercy. This is impossible. I don't know what to do." Kelly leaned back and let her head rest on the back of the chair. "That is all."

The room went back to quiet. "Thank you for saying that," Marie said to Kelly.

"I wanted to go first and get the crying out of the way, so my eyes wouldn't be too red for my interview." Kelly wiped the tears with her fingertips. A few people laughed softly.

Kelly's dilemma of justice versus mercy resounded with me. But something she said struck me as the room became quiet.

I wonder if any of that Robert Ray is left.

How could I know? He didn't give us much of a clue during his allocution. I thought about all the testimony we heard in the last week of the trial, how Robert Ray continued to manipulate those around him for his own benefit. He had even managed to flirt with a female prison guard and get small favors from her. She was fired for the inappropriate relationship and as a final indignity was forced to testify before us. A tight twinge pulsed in my gut.

I wonder if any of that Robert Ray is left.

"Well, c'mon now, someone else needs to go," Kelly said, her tears now dried. "If I have more crying to do, I need to get it done soon. Before my job interview, please!"

"I'll go next." Rick raised an open hand at a sharp angle up next to his face. "I know how you are feeling. I don't know what I'm going to do, either. As I see it, I'm damned if I do, damned if I don't." Rick was bent over in his chair, which was pushed back from the table. His elbows were on his knees, head barely higher than the table. He stared ahead at nothing in particular. "If I let him off with life in prison, what am I saying? Am I saying that this murder is no different than a typical murder? I don't believe that. He killed a witness. That's really bad, killing a witness."

Rick's voice trailed off as he spoke, the color draining from his face as he stared ahead. "But if I decide to kill him, and I'm not kidding myself, that's what this would be—I would be killing him." Rick spoke flatly, his voice revealing no emotion. He stayed bent over with his elbows on his knees. "I'm going to be wondering forever if I made the right choice. Could he be reformed in prison? Did he really have full control of what he was doing?"

Rick told us that the testimony of the psychiatrists and brain development experts connected with him. He regarded that evidence as the most scientific approach to understanding what make Robert Ray tick. "But in the end, Robert did something terribly evil. And I don't know if the psychiatric evidence can explain it away. Like I said, I'm damned if I do, and damned if I don't."

Rick apparently viewed himself as the one in the actual execution chamber, pulling the switch, so to speak. For a moment, I imagined myself in the observation room of the death chamber. Robert Ray is wheeled in, strapped to a gurney. His family is across the room, glaring at me. As the lethal drugs run through the tube into Robert's arm, his mom screams at me. "Killer!" She lunges at me as a guard holds her back.

I imagined leaving the prison, walking down a sidewalk lined with death penalty protestors. They boo and jeer. "You are no better than an animal! Blood lust! Savage!"

It would be so much easier to choose life in prison, I thought. I would never need to wonder if I made the right choice. I would never have scenes of a death chamber in my mind. And I could still comfort myself knowing that Robert Ray was getting a harsh punishment after all. He was going to die in jail either way, so why should I have to be responsible for it?

But something else Rick said caught my attention. This was not an ordinary murder. This was an execution of a witness in order to save maybe six years in jail. The crime was a direct hit to the justice system of my community, throwing the police and the district attorney's office into disarray and scaring witnesses in other cases. This murder was orchestrated carefully by Robert Ray to keep his own hands clean, and he coerced his family and close friends into becoming accomplices.

The result was his best friend was now on death row and many of his family in jail, too. Those who weren't in jail, like his wife and sisters-in-law, were compelled to testify under plea arrangements. Some of his family members even left the state to live in hiding. And there was the impact to the families of Javad and Vivian. This is what my imaginary death penalty protestors did not understand. The devastation caused by these murders cannot be distilled to a slogan on a cardboard sign. What am I saying to the community if I punish this outrageous act with the same punishment that might be given for the murder of a rival drug dealer?

In a flash, I remembered the moment when the prosecutor questioned me months before in individual juror interviews.

"Why do you think we have the death penalty in Colorado?"

"I believe the purpose of the death penalty is to punish especially heinous crimes. It is a statement that the state will only tolerate so much."

I need to make a statement, I thought, but did I have the courage to actually make that statement? Would I be willing to put my hand on the button and push it, killing Robert Ray, in order to make a *statement*? The tight twinge returned to my gut.

Why does this burden have to fall on me?

There were others in our group who seemed ready to live with the burden of choosing the death penalty. Dan was the first of them to speak. Dan was only a year away from retiring from his job in an auto body repair shop. He knew exactly how many days were left before he would be free to live his dream travelling the country in an RV, to come and go as he pleased, and do plenty of fishing.

Dan was a big bear of a man, his gray hair cut high and tight, like a soldier. Yet he always spoke gently and quietly. He had experienced tragedy in his life, losing his wife to cancer several years before.

Dan pulled a notecard from his shirt pocket. "I wrote a few things down, because at my advanced age, I'm likely to forget what I was going to say." Dan looked toward me, and I smiled at him. "Although I'm not quite as old as Mr. Hower."

A few jurors laughed softly at this reference to the lead prosecutor. Dan always sat immediately to my right, and I could see the notecard had a neat, bullet-point list of what he wanted to say.

"I grew up in a rough neighborhood, too, yet I did not become a criminal. When all that evidence was brought up about Chicago, I suppose most people focused on all the bad things that happened there." Dan looked up from his notecard for a moment and looked around the room. "But what I take away is how many of those witnesses— brought up by the defense team, mind you—also grew up on the South Side, and they aren't murderers. The defense brought in school teachers, coaches, firefighters, pastors, and some of Robert Ray's childhood friends. They all said it was hard to grow up in Chicago, but none of them are killers or even criminals. A lot of them actually have good jobs and are productive members of society. Robert Ray had his mother, uncles, grandmother, school teachers, and coaches all looking out for him as best they could. He wasn't thrown out on the streets to survive on his own. His teachers even said he was a promising student. So, I don't buy it, this idea that the South Side ruined him."

There was something in the way that Dan spoke that was calm and reassuring. He spoke quietly but confidently, as a man who lived a full life, overcoming many problems, and unafraid of what might be ahead. His warmth balanced the cold and clinical assessment that Rick had delivered a few minutes earlier.

Dan flipped over his note card. There was more writing on the back. "And trust me, I took quite a few knocks to the head when I was a kid. I'm not the smartest guy, and I've certainly made a few bone-headed decisions in my day. I wish I could blame it on head injuries. Robert Ray was capable of running a drug business and he was making a lot of money. He escalated things with Javad over a year. He didn't snap. I think his brain was working just fine. So, I don't buy the brain stuff either. Some of you may not agree with me, and that's okay. I'm just talking about my experience and how I feel about this. That's all."

Dan cleared his throat. He tapped his note card on the table a few times. Tears formed in his eyes. "I've thought a lot about those two beautiful young people. Their deaths were just so senseless." Dan's voice wavered an octave higher. "And that coward—what he did was not just murder them but attack the justice system itself. I've seen nothing to excuse it." Big Dan squeezed his eyes shut for a few seconds, trying to push the emotions down somewhere into the deep.

Dan never said how he was going to vote, but my guess from his demeanor was that he would vote for the death penalty. His words opened a floodgate of conversation among those who felt the same way. There was a lot of discussion about Chicago and head injuries. We went back over our notes and looked at the major points and counterpoints argued before us in the previous three weeks. The discussion went on for another hour before we took a break.

Shortly before our noon deadline, Steven announced that he "would like to say a few words." Like Dan, he pulled notes from his pocket. But unlike Dan's notes, these were not bullet point reminders of what he wanted to say. Steven had written his remarks in full, obviously having thought about his decision some time ago.

I glanced at the clock and over at Kelly, who was also looking at the clock, already thinking about leaving for her job interview. As Steven read his statement, she gathered her purse in her lap. She had a finger through the key ring of her car and she twisted it around and into the palm of her hand. Then Steven said something that caught my full attention.

"I just don't think that another killing is going to do any good," he said.

This is exactly how the defense team had summed up their arguments to us right before we left for deliberations: *another killing won't do any good.*

Steven kept reading from his paper. "Life in prison without parole is a harsh punishment. Robert Ray will never again be free. He won't be free to walk out in the beautiful mountain scenery of Colorado. He won't be free to eat his favorite meals. He will never again know the warmth of a woman's love."

Beautiful mountain scenery. The warmth of a woman's love.

These words jarred me. It seemed strange to hear them in a life-or-death discussion about punishing a double murder, like finding a beautiful Christmas ornament in a trash heap.

Vivian loved to hike in the mountains of Colorado. What about her? Javad loved Vivian with all his heart and was set to marry her. What about him? Who the hell cares that Robert Ray won't be free to take a hike or feel the warmth of a woman's love? He put Javad and Vivian in caskets six feet underground. What warmth and love will they find there? Steven continued to read but I was barely hearing. I realized now how I felt about this decision. The twinge in my gut returned and stabbed me sharply. I gripped the armrests on my chair. My hands slid along them, moist with sweat.

I don't think life in prison is enough.

Steven concluded by saying that the death penalty was too good for Robert Ray. It was the easy way out. Robert himself was probably hoping we would choose death for him. We should spare Robert's life, he said, because that way he would have to spend decade after miserable decade reflecting on the horribleness of his crimes. Plus, he said, putting Robert Ray on death row would make him a celebrity in the criminal world and bring him notoriety every time his case was in the news because of appeals and eventually his execution. "And for all these reasons, I think that life in prison is the more appropriate punishment." Steven folded his paper and put it back in his shirt pocket.

By then, Kelly was sitting at the edge of her seat. Noon exactly. She pushed her chair back from the table.

"Uh, Okay, well I guess that is all for today," I stammered. "On that note, have a great weekend and see you on Monday."

I walked in a line of jurors back to the parking lot, escorted by armed deputies. *A great weekend?* I nearly laughed thinking about how ridiculous that must have sounded. How could there be a great weekend now? I would have to dwell on all this for two more days, unable to say anything about it to anyone, putting the thoughts and realizations I just had on ice somehow. And we had ended the day with Steven's bombshell. He was set to vote for life in prison, making any revelations I had that day a moot point. If death was to be the penalty, we had to be unanimous, and it was clear now that we weren't. Further discussion might be interesting, but ultimately useless.

As I drove home, the words rattled around in my head: *beautiful mountain scenery. The warmth of a woman's love.* Steven's arguments about the death penalty were all valid, but this crime was so horrible and so damaging, I felt we had to punish it differently. The death penalty is the harshest sentence under Colorado law. If I truly believed that the crime was among the worst the state has seen, and the mitigating factors were not sufficient, then there was only one choice. While Steven's speech may have been jarring, it clarified what I believed.

Somewhere along Arapahoe Road as I drove west, the fog surrounding my decision finally dissolved, and I saw clearly what I was to do. Robert Ray must pay with his life for what he did.

I parked my car in the garage, turned off the engine, and sat for a moment, growing warm as the airflow stopped. I wasn't sure if I felt sad or angry. The twinge in my gut that started during Steven's speech returned and my palms grew moist with sweat again. The decision was not going to go my way. I felt like I had let Javad and his family down. Sweat formed on my forehead. I wanted to make the case for Javad. I felt somehow that I owed it to him, that he deserved it. I knew my arguments would ultimately fail, because we would not be unanimous. Still, someone needed to speak one more time for Javad and his family, and that someone would be me. I would give a speech of my own.

I started up my laptop on the dining room table and opened up a new page. I stared at the small piano across the room for a moment, kids' music books spread out across its dark wood top. Then all the thoughts, revelations, and anguish of the day came tumbling out onto the keyboard. I felt the sweat still there on my forehead and neck. Molly came down the stairs into the dining room, probably hearing me type.

"Are you Okay? Why are you back so soon?"

"Half-day today, we'll be back on Monday." I didn't pause my typing.

Molly moved around the table behind me. "What's going on. Work?"

"No. But there's something I must do."

Molly looked at me, concerned. A strand of her reddish-brown hair parted onto her forehead. "You seem…angry." Molly was not used to seeing any emotion out of me, much less anger.

"I don't know. I'm angry. I'm sad. I'm desperate." This was likely the first time I had admitted any of these emotions to my wife.

I turned to look up at Molly. She crouched a bit to see the laptop screen.

"Hey, don't read this. I don't want to get in trouble," I said.

She looked away from the screen. "Is there anything I can do?"

I closed the laptop and looked up at her for a moment. Molly took a half-step closer to me and placed her hand on my shoulder. I wrapped my arm around her waist and leaned into her from the chair. I took a breath and let out a shaky exhale. "It won't be much longer now, and this will all be over."

"Things will go back to normal." Molly leaned over the top of my head.

I thought for a moment. "I don't know if things will ever go back to normal."

fifteen
WHO AM I TO JUDGE?

Idid not want to sleep Friday night, afraid of what I might dream. Amazingly, I had never dreamed about the trial, or anyone involved in it, during all those weeks. If I had, the dream was not vivid and lasting enough to be remembered when I awoke. This seemed strange to me because my experience started out with a vision that occurred when I pulled the jury summons out of a stack of mail. Since then, nothing.

If a dream was to come, it probably would be this night, after our most emotional deliberations yet. Perhaps Javad and Vivian might appear as angry ghosts, bemoaning how we failed to get the full measure of justice for them. I can't dream if I don't sleep, I thought. I settled on the couch after my wife and kids went to bed and dialed in some mindless television.

Eventually, exhaustion overcame me, and I slept. I must have slumped over awkwardly on the couch, as I awoke around two in the morning with a dull, throbbing pain in my arm tucked beneath me. I struggled to realize where I was, my head heavy and my mouth sticky. I flicked off the television and negotiated the dark stairway to my room. My arm began to tingle with a hundred tiny needles as blood flow resumed, jolting me back to consciousness. I slipped into bed, trying not to disturb my wife. Now awake again, I laid in bed for another hour, my body wanting desperately to sleep but my mind fighting slumber and dreams. I stared at the ceiling and the closet door and finally succumbed, too exhausted to fight any more. No ghosts appeared, and I slept long into the morning.

Saturday dragged on heavy, slow, and sad with nothing particular to do. No family activities, no deadlines—a rare quiet Saturday. The other weekends during the trial were full of activities, especially with the kids, and the busyness helped to take my mind off the trial for a few hours. In contrast, that Saturday provided too much time to sit and think. About the decision I had made. About the reaction that would come when the trial was over. And most depressingly, about returning to work at a job, an entire career, that I had come to view as petty and pointless. As the Saturday wore on, I alternated between depression and anxiety. Anxious about the decision and the reaction, depressed about returning to "normal," whatever that would be for me.

I thought maybe a run would get the endorphins flowing again and clear my mind. I drove to a trailhead along the Highline Canal, which winds its way through the Denver area. The trail arcs gracefully through the prettiest neighborhoods, the trees parting at times to dramatic views of the mountains to the West.

I started running at a frenetic pace, far above my normal speed. The anxiety I had felt all day seemed to propel me forward. At first, it felt good to release the energy down through my body to my feet and into the ground, like electricity. I breathed heavily but steadily as I took a curve to the west. I only made it about a mile and a half, though, before exhaustion suddenly took over, and my legs became rubbery and my lungs scorched. I stopped along the edge of the trail, my shoes scuffing the dirt. I bent over and braced myself on my knees. I spit on the ground, breathing too rapidly even to swallow properly. After a half-minute or so, I pushed myself back upright and looked ahead.

The trail curved sharply to the north. Directly in front of me was a bench a few feet from the trail. It stood underneath a solitary cottonwood tree, crowned with a splash of new, light green leaves. The tree arched high over the bench, casting a scraggly shadow on the trail. I sat on the bench, facing west. The evening sunlight slanted across the mountains, thin and purple. The peaks cut a jagged ridgeline in the clear sky. I sat for a few minutes staring at the mountains, my heart rate and breathing finally slowing.

Am I really ready to do this?

I slumped forward again, my elbows on my knees. After ten weeks, I should have been ready. What more was there to do? The court asked me to make a life or death decision, and I had. Death.

I dwelt on the word: death. I thought of the finality of it. I knew that everyone would die someday, but this decision set the terms. The death penalty is normally a relatively humane way to die, drifting off with drugs delivered through a needle—certainly better than drowning in your own blood in the back of an ambulance. So why does the death penalty decision sting so much? The decision made a statement, a judgment, an utter rejection of a person. Robert Ray, a fellow human being, and his lawyers, family, and friends all pleaded with me to grant mercy, and I said no.

I struggled to sit upright on the bench. Nausea bubbled in my gut and I felt dizzy, my ears ringing slightly.

So why not show mercy?

It was a nagging and seductive question. At the very least, mercy would be an easy way out. I would never have to think about the death of Robert Ray again. Mercy is simply withholding a punishment that is deserved. Justice, though, is essential to society as well. Without it there is chaos. Without it the dignity of victims is diminished. Without it, we allow the criminal to determine the value of life and which life is worth more than another. Without it there can never really be equality. Because of these things, sometimes justice requires an extraordinarily harsh punishment.

How does God decide between justice and mercy?

I watched the sun dip close to the mountains, bits of dust visible in the light. The thought occurred to me: God delivers both justice and mercy, not one or the other. I am granted mercy by God because justice was delivered through the death of Christ. This was a truth I had known for most of my life, yet it became real to me for the first time ever on that park bench along the trail.

I stood up from the bench, wobbly for a moment, as the last slice of sun dipped below the mountains, sending broad rays upward from the purple peaks. I am not God, I thought to myself—probably the truest thought I've ever had.

I can't do both for this crime—I must pick one or the other.

The families of the victims wanted the ultimate punishment. The prosecution, representing the people, wanted the ultimate punishment. And I agreed with them. The crime was so serious, so shocking. The mitigation, while often compelling, was not enough. I had to choose, and it was as simple as that. Our imperfect, human system cannot do what God can do, to be both perfect in mercy and justice at once. I would vote for the full measure of justice at that moment, the only moment, it could ever be delivered.

The decision forced me to confront something about myself: I was out of balance when it came to mercy and judgment. Not in the criminal sense, but in the everyday interaction with others. Most of my life, since I became the ideal Christian boy, was focused on judgment. The experience of the trial had revealed this.

As I began a slow jog back toward home, I felt tremendously sad for all the times I had judged and condemned people, even if only in my own mind, when it was not necessary. "God," I whispered to myself, "I'm done trying to do your job. I've been so judgmental my entire life. Forgive me all those times in my life when I was a judge and didn't need to be. Forgive me for not showing mercy in the past when I should have. Help me to do the only job you ever asked me to do—love my neighbor."

sixteen
TWELVE BALLOTS

A s I drove to the courthouse on Monday, I rehearsed a little speech. Not the speech I felt compelled to deliver for Javad to the jury and planned to do later that morning. This speech I prepared for the press. At the first verdict a month before, they lined the back of the room, notebooks in hand, microphones at the ready. I knew they would be there again. Maybe they would descend on me in the parking lot, holding out a small forest of microphones before me. I knew they would want a comment. They would want to know why we didn't choose the death penalty. I felt that the public, so invested in the outcome, deserved at least a short explanation. As I drove, I repeated aloud my little statement several times:

I am proud of how we did our jobs these last two months. We were thorough and fair, and we agonized over our choices. This is the extraordinary aspect of our justice system: we put twelve strangers together and gave them these heavy decisions to make. The system is designed with safety in mind—safety in numbers. In the end, we each had to decide for ourselves what was right.

The vote was very close to deciding for the death penalty, but we were not quite unanimous. This means Robert Ray will get life in prison. Now we must all respect the decision and move ahead. We are grieved by this horrible crime against not only the victims but the justice system itself. We are profoundly sorry for the families of the victims and we wish them well as they try to move forward.

I didn't know how close the vote would be. Maybe nine to three, seeing that Kelly and Rick seemed on the fence, and Steven had indicated a vote for life in prison. At a minimum, it would be eleven to one. As I recited my little press statement, I struggled to keep the wording neutral and to keep from criticizing the decision as wrong. In my heart, I hated having to say these words. They sounded hollow to me, and I felt like a politician carefully parsing a statement, or a marketing expert putting a spin on bad news.

Back in the courthouse, the rest of the jury looked more beat-up than I'd ever seen before. Such bleary eyes. Such slow movement. A sticky tiredness hung over the room, clinging to everyone. My exhausted jurors clutched their coffee cups tightly. Apparently, none of us had a good night's sleep for a long time. The usual small talk about the events of the weekend was gone. We all took our seats silently as soon as everyone was present, as though to say, well, let's get this over and done. I was there for one reason now—to give my speech for Javad, in one last effort for what I believed to be the full measure of justice. What happened after that, I would deal with it when it happened, whatever it might be.

"I suggest we endure another round of deliberations," I told the group. "Then after that, we can decide if we are ready to vote."

As was our custom, we would let everyone have a chance to speak for however long they would like. As usual, I asked for a volunteer. Like she had done many times before, Kelly was the first to speak.

"I spent the entire weekend crying—the *entire* weekend."

I saw Marie smile and nod her head, the look on her face suggesting this happened to her as well.

"I cried about sentencing him to death. I cried about giving him mercy. Then I cried some more about sentencing him to death. Then I cried some more about giving him mercy." Kelly spoke plainly without any tears or hesitation. She sat firmly upright in her chair, calm and steady.

"Then I thought to myself, why I am I crying? I didn't put him in this position. I should be crying for the victims."

Kelly swiveled her chair to look out the window, leaning back and crossing her arms. A sliver of sunlight from the window illuminated some dust in the air.

"Well, I am done crying for Robert Ray. That's it. I am done thinking about him. I am done agonizing for him. I am done crying for him."

Kelly sat in her chair exuding a mix of quiet anger and tenacity. Her resolve was a thing of beauty. She fought to the end and finished the task. She had decided. She was done. The state, the defense, the judge—they had all thrown everything they had at her. And Kelly finished unshaken. I was proud of her.

"I would like to go next, unless anyone else would," I said. I wanted to build on the strength Kelly had shown. The others looked at me expectantly, so I stood up. I asked Greg to hand me the evidence folder that was full of pictures of Javad, pictures that Rhonda fields presented when she testified a few days before. As the jury watched me silently, I set up several pictures of Javad on the easel including the one of the "Sacrifice" tattoo on his back. Then I wrote the following on the easel pad, the marker squeaking on the paper:

COLORADO LAW
Punishment for 1st degree murder, after deliberation:
1. Death
2. Life imprisonment, no parole

I turned back to face the jury, standing next to Kelly who sat at the end of the table. My hands were trembling slightly as I picked up the papers with the words to my speech.

"We voted on Thursday that the murder of Vivian Wolfe was not aggravated enough for us to consider punishment, so that punishment defaulted to life in prison. Out of respect for that decision and the law, I will limit my comments to Javad only."

I looked up for a moment. I could see Rick out of the corner of my eye, immediately to my right. He was looking at me, his face expressionless.

"Javad studied Speech Communication at Colorado State. As you know, he wanted to be a lawyer or a lobbyist. I've written a speech in his honor. You are welcome to listen to it. But I'm not doing this for you. I'm doing it for him."

The pages fluttered in my fingers as I began to read,

"Ladies and Gentlemen of the jury, I must speak on behalf of those who believe that this crime deserves the death penalty. Even if my efforts fail, I owe this to Javad Marshall Fields and to the memory of his courage and strength. These will be my last comments of the deliberations. As the foreperson, it is my signature alone on the verdict form, but if we are not unanimous on the penalty, I must accept the decision anyway."

I cast a quick, sideways glance at Steven who was sitting to my left. Like Rick, he looked at me with no expression on his face, sitting upright in his chair. He was listening politely. He had no idea how his speech two days before had affected me. I continued,

"Life imprisonment is a severe penalty. This crime is more severe. Not every murder deserves the death penalty, but this is an extraordinary one. Killing a witness is a direct blow to our justice system and our community. It deserves the harshest punishment. It is undeniable that under Colorado law, the death penalty is the most severe punishment. Life in prison will be interpreted as the second-worst punishment. It will raise a valid question: just what is worthy of our most extreme punishment? Life in prison says we believe Robert Ray is less culpable than Sir Mario Owens for the same crime. What did Owens have to gain doing Robert's dirty work for him? How can he be the only one deserving of death for killing a witness? We should not play reverse psychology with the law, trying to figure out what punishment Robert Ray fears most. Our job is to decide what is most appropriate for the crime regardless of what he wants."

I paused for a moment to catch my breath, looking down at the "Sacrifice" photo on the easel. When I looked back up, I noticed Lois looking intently at me, nodding her head slowly. Her look made me feel courageous, knowing my words connected with at least one other person.

"If we put Robert Ray on death row, he will have many years to get his life in order during appeals. He can reflect on what he did, express his sorrow, ask forgiveness, and get his affairs in order. Javad received no appeal, was given no chance to say goodbye, and died in the back seat of his car, choking on his own blood and gasping for breath as air rushed from his punctured lungs so fast it formed bubbles on the skin of his chest.

"And what if we sentence Robert Ray to life imprisonment? With his good behavior and charming demeanor, he will earn a large variety of privileges. He will be able to exercise on the prison yard basketball court. He will enjoy television, radio, and newspapers, and perhaps see the Broncos win another Super Bowl. Yes, even in prison, there is some small measure of hope. He will enjoy music, movies, and books from the library. He will enjoy continued learning and even take college courses. Perhaps he will obtain his degree in wildlife biology like he said he wanted to when he was in high school. He could even buy a Mother's Day card.

"How much would Rhonda Fields pay now for those privileges to be extended to her son? How much would she pay for one more conversation with him? What price would she pay to see Javad play basketball in the Marshall's backyard? How much is it worth for another smile from him at his nieces' antics? I daresay she would pay with her own life. She would trade places with Javad in a heartbeat for just one of these privileges that Robert Ray will enjoy the rest of his life.

"Javad died because he dared to obey the law. He stayed true to his commitment to testify when every other witness ran away in fear. How dare we dishonor that sacrifice and the sacrifice of his family with the second-worst punishment!"

My voice rose with that last sentence. I looked up again toward Lois, afraid to look at Steven or Rick. I didn't want to lose heart if I saw them reacting negatively.

"Perhaps Robert Ray's moral code was warped by a catastrophic childhood. Perhaps I would use this to mitigate his crime if only he showed sincere remorse. Since Lowry Park, he has had a year of freedom and four years of incarceration to consider right and wrong compared to his choices. Five years to learn what a lawful, moral society is like, complete with anger management classes for which he earned top grades and high praise from the Department of Corrections. Yet after years of sitting in jail, he wrote on his jail cell wall: 'Fuck Arapahoe County.' And what of his big opportunity to address us at the end of the trial? When he realized 'the moms' were not present, how did he react? I quote: 'Why the fuck am I even standing here?' Because, Mr. Ray, you have a chance to tell us, the people about to judge you, how you truly feel. And apparently, I can summarize his feelings as: fuck you, fuck all of you."

My voice was quivering. How long had I been speaking? I turned a page and saw another sea of words. I felt awkward as I stood there and caught my breath. Was I overdoing it? The jury, though, listened patiently and quietly, watching me intently. I realized this was it, the last things I would say in our deliberations. The thought made me suddenly feel nervous, dizzy. So many hours, days, weeks of my life being poured into this trial. My eyes moistened with tears.

"Despite all that, Robert Ray is a human being. I saw glimpses of his humanity more than once. He loves his family. A death penalty decision would be very sad for all of them. Why must I make this awful choice? He's never harmed me. Yet here I am, an ordinary citizen forced to make the extraordinary choice. Robert Ray knew right from wrong. He was smart enough to keep his own body clean of drugs and alcohol. He chose to involve his family in his crimes. He was more than willing to smear the blood of Javad Fields all over his friends and family while he kept himself safe from the messy scene, hiding behind a contrived alibi. It isn't fair, and now full justice is required.

"I imagine that years from now people will ask me why I voted to put a man on death row. What about mercy? What about reform? What about forgiveness? What about civility? Doubtless they'll have lots of arguments about why the death penalty is wrong. Then they'll look at me with a mixture of pity and contempt, as though I'm the barbarian. They'll regard me as the killer. It will be easy for them to do this because years from now they won't remember the victims. They won't remember the crime. The shock to the justice system. The enormous wave of damage done to literally hundreds of people. They will make their breezy pronouncements and platitudes without having considered a single word of the one hundred and eleven witnesses I heard. Or a single instruction of law. Or any thought for the realities of evil. They'll have the luxury of judging me without having done any of my work.

"On death row, Robert Ray will have ample opportunity to receive grace and forgiveness and be transformed by it. His legal team will appeal for years to the highest courts in the land. But this moment right now, in this cramped little jury room, is our only chance, the people's only chance, the victim's only chance, to deliver the most extraordinary justice for the most extraordinary crime."

I drew in another shaky breath and exhaled. I folded my pages in half. Someone was clapping. I looked up. It was Lois Butler, the retired high school principal. "That was perfect," she said. "Bravo, Carl. That took guts. And you managed to say exactly what I am feeling. It's like you knew exactly what I was thinking, and you put it into words better than I ever could have."

I could see Greg, James, and Vicki at the far end of the table. I didn't look around to see if there were other reactions.

I said, "thank you," but just barely, my voice raspy and weak. I needed water. I sat down and took a long drink from my water bottle. I didn't feel triumphant. I wasn't happy or sad or anything. I was just—*done*.

Several other jurors spoke after I did. I didn't keep track of how many spoke or even what they said entirely. I didn't care. I had done what I came to do that day. I had nothing more to say, and I had nothing left I wanted to hear. I was completely empty.

"That was for you, Javad," I said to myself, as though praying, "I don't know if it was enough, but I hope you are proud anyway."

◆ ◆ ◆

"Does anyone want to say anything more?" I was doing my usual pre-vote check, something I had done during our deliberations at least a dozen times. About an hour had passed since my speech. We had taken a break and returned to the jury room. "Does anyone have any questions?" I paused for about twenty seconds. "Does anyone want any more time or need anything else?" I waited again. I wanted to be sure that there was nothing else, that we were all finished with speeches, questions, tirades, and tears. Silence enveloped us, as we all stared at the table, the window, or the door—anything but each other. "Okay then. Please take out the ballot from your folders. Take as long as you want to vote. I mean that—as long as you want. We can be here all day and beyond if you need it."

I marked my ballot with an "x" for the death penalty and flipped the page over face down on the table in front of me. I was anticipating this vote to take an hour, or maybe more. I stood up quietly and walked into the adjacent restroom. When I left the restroom a minute or two later, I was surprised to find a stack of ballots, face down on top of mine. I counted them without looking at what the votes were. There were twelve ballots. I looked up, surprised. The jurors were looking back at me, quite nonchalantly.

"Well, aren't you going to tally them?" Rebecca asked me from across the table.

"Yes. Yes, I am. Just give me a minute."

I turned around and stepped over to the small table against the wall of the jury room. I didn't want to count the ballots with everyone staring at me. With my back to the jury, I looked at each ballot. I felt faint and leaned against the wall. I looked at each one again. Could I believe what I was seeing? "Rebecca, could you come over here and check these?" I asked. This was also a routine we had started with every vote, which, given the number of criminal counts in the case, was at least fourteen. I would count the ballots and Rebecca would double-check them.

Rebecca edged around the table and over to me.

I whispered to her, "I'm not sure I can trust my own eyes here. I think it's unanimous." I watched as Rebecca thumbed through each page, flipping them down onto the table as if she was dealing cards.

"Yes, unanimous," she whispered back to me. I watched as she walked back to her chair and sat down, her face expressionless. There was total quiet in the room.

"We are unanimous," I said, "Robert Ray is sentenced to death for the murder of Javad Marshall Fields."

And that was it. In our previous deliberations a month earlier, when we found Robert Ray guilty of the murders, the verdict came with an outpouring of tears and grief. This time, the jury simply watched in silence as I marked and signed the official verdict form. The sound of the pen scratching the paper was louder than anything else at that moment. I twisted my pen shut and dropped it onto my notebook.

Big Dan extended his right hand to me, the other he placed on my shoulder. I reached out to grasp his hand. He shook it firmly. "We did it," he said. "The job is done! I am so glad you were our leader, Carl." Then turning to the rest of the group, still grasping my hand, he said, "And I have never been prouder to be associated with a group of people than I am with all of you."

I looked over at Greg, sitting in his usual spot at the end of the table. I don't know why the two-way radio for the bailiff was always down on his end. "Greg, the radio," I said. He slid it across the table to me. I picked it up and pressed the microphone switch. "Bailiff, please come to the jury room."

◆　◆　◆

In Hollywood courtroom dramas, the verdict scenes are always very intense. The jury foreperson reads the verdict, pausing for effect right before the final words. The defendant either collapses into a chair with relief or is led sputtering mad out of the courtroom. The people in the gallery gasp in astonishment when the verdict is announced. Sometimes there is even yelling, wails, or shrieks. The judge bangs the gavel on the desk, "Order! There will be order in my court!"

The final verdict reading in the case of *People vs. Robert Ray* could not have been more different than the Hollywood stereotype. The proceedings were clinical, even cold, by comparison. The room was packed, with every seat filled and people standing along the walls. I was amazed that so many people in such a small space could be so quiet. Judge Rafferty must have given them a stern warning, like he had done for our first verdict. As before, the prosecution team crowded together at their table, but now it was clear of papers and books. Like she did during the first verdict, the lead detective folded her hands together and rested her forehead on them as though in silent prayer, her eyes closed.

At first, I stared down at my feet, intensely aware that the eyes of everyone were on me. Then I decided that, no, I would not look away as though I was the guilty one. We had done our job, and I was proud of how we did it. Proud of the effort, the agony, and the care that we took. We had nothing to be ashamed of. I had nothing to be ashamed of. I lifted my head and looked around the room, back at those staring at me. Their eyes quickly turned down from my gaze. The judge read the verdict in a monotone clip. I looked to my left and saw Rhonda Fields, Javad's mother. She looked directly at me, her face beaming. She seemed assured and not at all surprised.

The judge then questioned each of us individually. "Juror 12, was this and is this your verdict."

"Yes." My voice was clear. My throat felt relaxed, my eyes dry.

After each juror was asked to confirm the vote, the bailiff called out, "All rise." This was our signal that we could leave now. We the jury stood up and walked out of the courtroom for the last time, in complete silence.

I glanced over my left shoulder as I neared the door. I saw the defendant standing with his hands clasped at the waist in front of him. As usual, there was no expression on his face.

We stood in the jury room and waited for the bailiff to tell us it was safe to leave. A few jurors cried softly as we said goodbye. We hugged each other, shook hands, and promised to stay in touch. Vicki had put together a list of all our phone numbers and email addresses.

Kelly walked across the room and embraced me tightly for a moment. We didn't speak. I wanted to tell her about my vision, how I had seen her before we even met. That I saw the role she would have in our jury room before we were chosen. But the end of the trial was overwhelming enough, and I didn't want to startle her with some strange story about visions.

I had taken a long time to get comfortable with the vision. I had tried over the weeks to convince myself that it was just a trick of the mind, a coincidence. But now, looking back, I wondered if God was using the experience. Was He was trying to show me he could intervene in my life? I had thought of God before as the one who abandoned me despite my youthful life of righteousness. This trial was the first time I had recognized that I needed God and at last asked for His intervention.

The final part of my vision was a glimpse of a waiting press, cameras, microphones, and lights. I knew that would be next for me, and I felt prepared. I finally believed I had proven myself. I could make a big decision and lead others through the process. I could stand up and speak for those who had no voice.

After about twenty minutes, the bailiff appeared in the room along with Judge Rafferty. The judge thanked us all for our work and told us we could leave whenever we wanted. He gave us each a thin stack of papers. On top was a certificate of appreciation with the State of Colorado seal on it. Beneath that I found a photocopied article about the history of juries in America, as though we still needed to be convinced of our role in the justice system. Finally, a letter from the Arapahoe Mental Health Center that offered a free psychotherapy session if we needed help with "debriefing" after the trial.

"I think this means that the trial has made us certifiably crazy," Greg joked.

Judge Rafferty then told us that if we wanted, we could go back into the courtroom. The family members of the victims wanted to meet us, and so did the prosecution team. The defense lawyers and the defendant had already left.

Along with a few other jurors, I walked back into the courtroom one last time. This time, I felt as though I was walking into a reception, with the room full of people talking, standing clustered in small groups.

Rhonda Fields saw me enter the room and strode purposefully up to meet me. She shook my hand and said, "Thank you for your courage and your service. This means everything to me." She threw her arms around my shoulders and hugged me.

A line of Javad and Vivian's family members circled me. People with notebooks and microphones hovered by my elbows, leaning in to see and hear what was happening. I was mobbed. One person after another, pictures of Javad and Vivian pinned to their clothing, came up to me and shook my hand or gave me a hug. Most of them didn't say anything. They just looked me in the eye, tears streaming down their faces. Some mouthed a silent "thank you." With each handshake and hug, I felt peace falling upon me. Every touch from a grateful family member passed to me an absolution for the terrible thing I had to do, for sending a man to death row.

When Christine Wolfe, Vivian's mother, came up to me, I struggled to hold back my own tears.

"I am sorry we could not deliver the verdict you wanted." The crew with notebooks and microphones pressed in on us. "I'm sorry we couldn't do the same for your daughter as we did for Javad. This was very difficult for us. I'm glad you are here today so I can tell you that we all admire Vivian and we are so sorry she is gone."

Christine took my hand and nodded her head gently. "Thank you for trying your best."

I felt someone grab me around my waist. I looked down to see that Javad's grandmother had worked her way through the crowd and was hugging me. She stood barely chest-high to me. She did not look up or say anything. Just a gentle hug. She was wearing a black dress with fabric covered in some sort of sequins or sparkles. When she turned and hobbled away, pulling her oxygen bottle behind her, I noticed that my shirt had a small streak of sparkles.

"Sir, can I get a statement? Denver Post." The voice came from one of the reporters now gathered in front of me. The final part of my vision was complete. Everything I had seen that afternoon months before the trial had now happened.

"This sentence was very difficult because we weighed the destruction and pain that was put on the families against the act of taking another man's life for causing these murders. I can honestly say we were twelve blank slates when we began. Gregory Vann is the forgotten ghost in all of this. The sentence is very much prompted by the defendant's attempt to escape prosecution for that murder. We had to stand up against the killing of a witness."

Several of the reporters began to ask questions all at once. I put my hand up. "I'll be right back." I had seen someone in the room I wanted to talk to.

It was Reverend Fulman, the last person to testify on behalf of Robert Ray. The one who warned us that we were not in any position to judge. He was the only person left in the room that was an advocate of Robert Ray. All of Ray's family and lawyers had long since gone, but Reverend Fulman stood there the entire time since we had returned to the courtroom, silently observing. As I approached him, he nodded at me, as though he already knew who I was.

"I was praying for you."

"Thanks. All of us on the jury appreciate it."

"No, not just the jury, but you specifically. Judgment is a heavy burden to bear. You were struggling with it."

He said this with warmth and compassion, not like a preacher who wanted to tell me, "See I told you so."

I looked at him for a second, this thin, tall man with glasses, his hair parted and combed neatly away from his forehead. How much did this man know about me? Were my struggles evident on my face during the trial? Did he make a lucky guess? Or had his prayers led to some divine revelation about me? I decided at that moment, it didn't matter. I extended my hand to him, and he grasped it. "You were right," I replied at last. "What you said from the witness stand. From now on, I'm leaving the judging to God."

An Epilogue in Three Scenes

I stood in the back of the room, leaning against the wall. More than a hundred people were seated in front of me. Several news cameras were setup on tripods near the front of the room, capturing video of the speakers, most of them local elected officials, who took turns addressing the audience. We had gathered to dedicate a new community center for the Fields Foundation, a charity setup in honor of Javad and Vivian. The community center sits on Dayton Street, the same street where Javad and Vivian were murdered nine years before, and only a mile away from Lowry Park, where Greg Vann died.

The Fields Foundation started as a scholarship fund, supplying more than two dozen high school graduates from Aurora with scholarships to Colorado State University, the *alma mater* of both Javad and Vivian. Now the Foundation is more than a scholarship fund. It is a place where people from Aurora can get health care, job training, and childcare. The crowd attending the dedication marveled at how so much good could be born from such tragedy and evil.

Five years before I stood in that crowded dedication ceremony, I arrived home from the last day of the trial in a daze. I took more than two hours to drive home that day, unsure that I was ready to emerge from my car into the real world again and into the life I had left behind for ten weeks. I drove up and down the streets of Arapahoe County, stopping several times in parking lots just to sit alone where nobody knew I was. Where nobody could say anything to me.

I turned on the radio and heard a news report about our decision and the death penalty. A reporter quoted me. I wondered what I was going to do now. Should I try to forget the entire ordeal and never speak of it again? Could that even be possible?

Back at home, I went to change into more comfortable clothes. As I hung up my courtroom clothes in the closet, I noticed a postcard in a back pocket of my pants. It was a brochure for the Fields-Wolfe Memorial Fund, announcing a golf tournament to raise funds for scholarships in Javad and Vivian's honor. Then I remembered that Rhonda Fields, Javad's mother, handed this to me when we talked in the courtroom after the trial. I must have slipped it into my pocket and then forgot about it.

I stared at the brochure for a moment. It had an elegant "J&V" script logo above a golf course scene, green grass, and cottonwood trees set against a blue Colorado sky. I remembered the testimony of how Javad earned money by caddying at a golf club in the summers. Javad and Vivian were also pictured on the brochure, a photo of them I had seen countless times now. In the picture, Javad wore a black cap and gown at graduation, his arm around Vivian.

I stood there in front of my closet for a minute longer before finally sitting quietly on the bed, slumped over, leaning with my elbows on my knees. I realized that I was about to make another decision. What was I going to do with this experience after all the chaos, death, tears, and grief I had witnessed? After the life-and-death choices I had made and their eternal consequences? It seemed to me that I could indeed try to forget it all and immerse myself again in the world of computer software—the job I was about to return to. I could try to stuff everything into a deep hole somewhere and bury it—or I could get involved. I could do something more. Maybe I could volunteer at this fund-raiser. Maybe I could donate money. Maybe somehow, I could make *something* positive out of all this.

I set the brochure on my nightstand, Javad and Vivian looking out at me from next to my alarm clock. I wasn't sure what that something would be, or what it would look like, but I knew one thing at that moment; I wanted to open up. I wanted to talk. I wanted to give. I wanted some good to come from the all the tragedy and trial.

◆　◆　◆

"I had a long talk with Jamie today." Molly sat near me on the couch—the new brown leather one we had just bought. Six years had passed since the end of the trial. We got rid of the hunter-green couch we had owned since early in our marriage—the one that hosted some of our most difficult and tear-stained outbursts.

"Jamie—she's your coworker?"

"Yeah. She and Jake are really going through it." Molly set a mug on the coffee table in front of us. "I don't know if their marriage can survive."

I looked up from the mug on the table and caught our reflection in the glass patio door. There we were, sitting on a couch and discussing a marriage. Only this time it wasn't ours. I broke my gaze with our reflection. "What seems to be their problem?"

Molly paused for a few seconds and then looked up at me. A very slight smile turned up the corner of her mouth. Not an amused smile.

A knowing one. "Actually, they are very much like you and me. Same problems. They remind me of us."

"You told them about our problems? That must have been a long conversation."

Molly smiled. She looked down at the mug on the table and pulled her legs up underneath her on the couch. This couch was sized more to fit my six-foot-four frame—her feet barely reached the floor when she sat. "Yeah—it was a long conversation. But I told them if we can make it, so can they. Almost twenty years now."

I looked intently at my wife for a few moments. I knew we had both gotten older, but she still looked like she did when I first fell in love. The same reddish-brown hair, styled short. The same green eyes, smooth skin, delicate chin. I realized I was getting a good deal.

Molly looked up, now aware that I was looking at her. "What?"

"You know, I just realized I don't care that you told another person all about our problems."

"Actually, Carl, it makes you more likeable when people know the real you."

"Well, years ago I didn't like it when people knew about my faults and doubts, especially the church. I was afraid of being judged. I worried about what people would think of me. There's a lot of contrast between the righteous reputation I had and what my faith was really like."

Molly took a sip from the mug. "I think you and I will have a ministry someday. There are a lot of couples who can relate to what we've been through, and I think we could be very useful to them. I can see us speaking to a lot of people."

I pondered what my wife had just said. I moved closer to her on the couch and put my arms around her shoulders. "But we still struggle with things—I'm not sure we'll ever be done with all our problems," I said.

"I'm actually content." Molly leaned her head onto my shoulder.

"And we're still together, working on things, and moving forward. And that's the important thing."

◆　◆　◆

In March of 2014, five years after the trial, I found myself wandering in the desert. I wasn't exactly wandering. More like staggering. But I was in a desert—the White Sands of New Mexico, about 30 miles north of the Mexico border. I went there to run a marathon, 26.2 miles in the Bataan Memorial Death March. Several thousand others attempted this with me.

It is one of the most difficult marathons in America. It takes most people all day to finish. The Army administers the race and provides aid stations about every two miles. The runners overwhelmed the aid stations, taking off their shoes to dump the sand out. The dry desert air gave us a deep blue sky with no clouds to provide even a moment's relief from the sun.

At mile 21, I entered an area called "the pit," a patch of ankle-deep, coarse sand that stretches for a mile up a hillside, which, aside from the sand, was covered in Yucca, cactus, and rocks. Running on a soft, sandy surface for so many miles is surprisingly damaging. The soft surface caused my ankles, knees, and hips to move in ways they normally don't on harder surfaces. My steps became short and choppy, like I was stabbing the ground with my toes, sand flying up over my shoes.

I'm not sure that what I was doing could be considered "running" at that point because I wasn't moving much faster than a walk. I started walking up the hillside to save energy. When I tried to start running again, my ankles and lower legs tightened, and each footfall sent a jolt of pain up my legs to my hips. I would have to walk most of the remaining course.

Despite the slow progress and the pain, though, I knew I would finish this race. I had the confidence that came with finishing nine other marathons in the previous five years. But more importantly, I knew to take a slow and steady pace, resisting the temptation early in the run to go fast. I had some energy left, enough to power through to the end. My previous experiences at marathon running weren't always this way.

A few years before my trial experience, I started running to reinvigorate my health and get back in shape. I thought of running as a quick way to lose some weight. I didn't expect to like it. But soon I worked my way from 5K runs to 10K to half marathons and finally a full marathon. In fact, I ran a marathon during the trial. In late 2008, a month or so before I received my jury summons in the mail, I started training to run a marathon in Oklahoma City scheduled for April of 2009. This, of course, ended up being right in the middle of the trial. I asked the judge if I could still leave town to run it, over a weekend. He agreed, and so off I went.

The marathon was a disaster. By then, I was so physically and mentally drained from the trial, that by mile seven (out of twenty-six), I could tell trouble was coming. I felt heavy and sluggish. I pressed on anyway, and by mile fourteen, I was flailing in a violent headwind, out of energy. I braced my upper body with hands on my hips and started walking. With a sickening sensation in my gut, I realized it would take hours to walk the final twelve miles. I decided I would run for a minute and then walk for two. I repeated this over and over, my feet often scuffing the pavement, until I finally reached the finish line six hours after I started.

I had no time to recover, needing to get home that night in order to be back at the trial the next morning. I asked for a bag of ice at an airport restaurant, and I sat at the boarding area with my bare, swollen feet pressed against the ice. Two toenails were blackened from being pounded into the front of my shoes. My feet hurt too much to put my shoes back on, so I boarded the airplane in stocking feet, the flight attendant looking at me and my bag of ice suspiciously as I limped down the aisle.

Fortunately for my fellow passengers, I had managed to get a two-minute shower at the hotel, the manager taking pity on me and letting me check out late. I buckled in for the flight and assured myself I would never run a marathon again. Maybe never run even another mile again. But five years later, I was in the White Sands desert finishing my tenth marathon. Since the trial, I have run over 6,000 miles.

Running—slow running over long distances—has become a metaphor for my life. Running is a useful way for me to view the world and my faith since the trial. Successful endurance running is a balancing act between two competing ideals: obsession and relaxation.

I've learned that obsession with detail is important to endurance running. A sock that doesn't fit quite right or a small nagging pain is tolerable for a mile or two. But after twenty miles, even small problems like these cause painful blisters or injuries that leave me hobbling in pain for days and even weeks following a race. Further, I've learned that obsession with finishing a run is crucial, too. Many times, I have wanted to give up in the middle of a difficult run, but I kept going, sometimes out of sheer stubbornness not to be seen as a failure.

In a sense, this is what I was like when I was the ideal Christian young man, so many years ago. I obsessed over every rule and regulation of evangelical Christianity. I refused to give in to anything or anyone that did not adhere to the black-and-white view I had of scripture. Then I learned that perfection is not attainable in life or in endurance running. This is where the relaxation part comes in.

At some point, our human nature, or simple exhaustion, causes us to break down or make a mistake. I have often changed my goals and plans in the middle of a marathon because the conditions had changed or because my health was not as strong as I thought. It is a humbling thing to do, to slow down, especially when other runners who don't seem as fit or athletic as I am pass me up. But the ability to relax is so important. I have had to listen to my body and let go of what I thought was the ideal plan or goal. I was once passed at the 25-mile mark by a little old lady who looked to be about 70 years old. Humbling.

I started my first marathon with the goal of finishing in less than four hours. For an amateur athlete like me, especially a big guy (I'm 6-foot-4 and about 220 pounds), this is a very respectable time, and a mark most amateurs aim to beat. But halfway through the 26.2 miles, I realized I could not do it. I would not break the four-hour barrier. The course was too tough, and I was not rested and did not have adequate nutrition to power through "the wall"—the point of a marathon where the muscles run out of glucose to power them and instead must burn the energy stored in fat, a painful and slow process that makes every muscle in the legs quiver.

If I tried to keep a four-hour pace, I would soon collapse. What good would that do? To finish the race slowly and humbly is better than to flame out in a blaze of speed. I had to let go of the goal, and I finished twenty minutes slower than I had hoped. At four hours, I still had two miles to go. In the ten marathons since then, I've never come close to breaking four hours, but I have finished every time, often in adverse or brutally difficult conditions.

I'm not saying that people should give up on their goals or stop improving, but I have learned to slow down. To listen. To be humbler. To be willing to change my long-held opinions. Most of all, I have learned to stop trying to get everyone to see things my way. I'm in the race for the distance.

I rarely take a hard line on anything anymore. Whether it is politics or the moral teachings of evangelical Christianity. My faith is more resilient. It can survive a discussion on evolution, or someone claiming that parts of the Bible are allegorical and not literal. I can enjoy and learn from my Christian sisters and brothers whether they are gay or straight. I no longer feel the need to rush in to defend the faith against every criticism. More importantly, I no longer need to defend myself.

My outlook has softened, especially toward other people—even those who I would have judged and written-off as failures or sinners in the past. I ask a different question now. Instead of wondering, "Are you right with God?" I ask, "What can I do to help?"

When I run, I often think about Javad. I want to be as courageous as he was. I want to live without fear and with a reputation for kindness. I often run by the bench along the Highline Canal, the place where I came to grips with judgment the day before the final verdict. Every time I do, I stop there, even if just for a moment. I ask God for courage. I gaze west toward the mountains and I picture Javad, Vivian, and Greg in their prime. I imagine them surrounded by friends who are gathered with laughter and music. Then I turn back to the trail, take a step, and start to run.

ACKNOWLEDGMENTS

The eleven other members of my jury served the community and the justice system with great diligence, compassion, and respect for everyone. Their service was not only a sacrifice of time. Many suffered financially. Some even lost their health in all the anguish. During the appeals process, this yet unpublished book added to their burden as several were called to testify on my behalf. They all deserve respect and gratitude and they certainly have mine.

This book would be a hopeless mess without Shari Caudron, an expert memoir coach who saw the potential of my story and pushed me to realize it. Her advice and encouragement helped me turn a wandering, cathartic exercise into a story with meaning and emotion.

K.B. Jensen led the publishing process and put together a team of editors, designers, lawyers, marketers, and everything else needed by Golden Elm Press to take this manuscript that difficult last mile. I appreciate the care and pride the entire team gave my story.

To the Fields and Wolfe families—I wish we could have met some other way. Your service to the community since that terrible day is an honor to your children and an inspiration to us all.

ABOUT THE AUTHOR

Authoring a book such as this one was completely unexpected for Carl Dubler, as was his experience with a double-murder case. Carl is a highly-regarded veteran of the computer software industry, and his articles and presentations on software have reached tens of thousands of people. But the engineering requirements and mathematical algorithms of software leave little room for emotion or nebulous feelings, so writing a memoir proved to be the biggest challenge Carl has ever faced. He and his wife have raised two children in Colorado, his life-long home. He is an expert outdoorsman and has led many groups of young people through backcountry adventures in all seasons. For more information or to request Carl for a speaking engagement or book club, visit www.carldubler.com.